Dear Young Friend

Dear Young Friend

Letters from American Presidents
to Children

RODELLE WEINTRAUB *and* **STANLEY WEINTRAUB**

STACKPOLE
BOOKS

Copyright © 2000 by Stanley Weintraub and Rodelle Weintraub.

Published by
STACKPOLE BOOKS
5067 Ritter Road
Mechanicsburg, PA 17055
www.stackpolebooks.com

All rights reserved, including the right to reproduce this book or portions thereof in any form or by any means, electronic or mechanical, including photocopying, recording, or by any information storage and retrieval system, without permission in writing from the publisher. All inquiries should be addressed to Stackpole Books, 5067 Ritter Road, Mechanicsburg, Pennsylvania 17055.

Printed in the United States of America

10 9 8 7 6 5 4 3 2 1

FIRST EDITION

Library of Congress Cataloging-in-Publication Data

Weintraub, Rodelle.
    Dear young friend : letters from American presidents to children / Rodelle Weintraub and Stanley Weintraub.— 1st ed.
        p. cm.
    Includes bibliographical references and index.
    ISBN 0-8117-0489-0
        1. Presidents—United States—Correspondence. 2. Children—United States—Correspondence. I. Weintraub, Stanley, 1929– II. Title.

E176.1.W368 2000
973′.09′9—dc21

00-022215

Contents

Introduction, vii
Note on Texts, xiii

Chapter One
THE ARISTOCRATIC PRESIDENCY, 1789–1861
page 1

George Washington (1789–1797), *1*
John Adams (1797–1801), *10*
Thomas Jefferson (1801–1809), *20*
John Quincy Adams (1825–1829), *32*
Andrew Jackson (1829–1837), *39*
Martin Van Buren (1837–1841), *50*
John Tyler (1841–1845), *54*
James Polk (1845–1849), *64*
Millard Fillmore (1850–1853), *68*
Franklin Pierce (1853–1857), *73*
James Buchanan (1857–1861), *77*

Chapter Two
THE DEMOCRATIZED PRESIDENCY, 1861–1901
page 83

Abraham Lincoln (1861–1865), *84*
Andrew Johnson (1865–1869), *88*

Ulysses S. Grant (1869–1877), *93*
Rutherford B. Hayes (1877–1881), *95*
James A. Garfield (1881), *98*
Chester Alan Arthur (1881–1885), *104*
Grover Cleveland (1885–1889, 1893–1897), *105*
Benjamin Harrison (1889–1893), *107*
William McKinley (1897–1901), *109*

Chapter Three
THE "BULLY PULPIT" PRESIDENCY, 1901–1953
page 113

Theodore Roosevelt (1901–1909), *114*
William H. Taft (1909–1913), *121*
Woodrow Wilson (1913–1921), *126*
Warren G. Harding (1921–1923), *130*
Calvin Coolidge (1923–1929), *134*
Herbert Hoover (1929–1933), *137*
Franklin Delano Roosevelt (1933–1945), *141*
Harry S. Truman (1945–1953), *147*

Chapter Four
THE MASS MEDIA PRESIDENCY, 1953–1974
page 155

Dwight D. Eisenhower (1953–1961), *155*
John F. Kennedy (1961–1963), *163*
Lyndon B. Johnson (1963–1969), *168*
Richard M. Nixon (1969–1974), *179*

Afterword: Post-Nixon, 1974–, *185*

Sources, 189

Introduction

George Washington began the practice, and few presidents since have not continued writing to young people. From as early as the father of our country to as recently as John Kennedy, many presidents addressed their youthful correspondents, especially in matters of childhood concern, as "Dear Young Friend." In letters to children (and we use the term to encompass young people who were legally minors), presidents often confided political thoughts and personal feelings that they seldom if ever confessed to their peers. Dwight Eisenhower even answered a girl's request for his views for her school newspaper with a revealing letter, which he then had stamped *confidential* and declared was not meant for print. In their letters, too, American presidents tended to be well aware of their role-model status, and this aspect of their personalities often emerges, sometimes amusingly, sometimes forbiddingly. Ranging from the perfunctory to the preachy, these letters illuminate presidential personality from an unfamiliar perspective.

As recently as the presidency of William McKinley, who died in office in 1900, the task of handling the White House mail was relatively simple. The volume of incoming mail was small, and McKinley would often tell a clerk, "Oh, write him thus and so. You know how to say it." Earlier presidents usually went through their own mail, and answered much of it themselves, often—in the era before typewriters, copy machines, and word processors—seeing to it that a copy was made on a letterpress or reproduced by hand in a letterbook. John Quincy Adams's wife, Louisa, sometimes performed that task for her husband, especially for his private correspondence, and may have prevented some awkward repercussions from his acerbic personality by discreetly copying a letter into her husband's records but not sending it. The Adams children received enough hortatory mail from their father not to miss an occasional verbal lashing.

Much of the early correspondence from American presidents to children is to young people in the presidential family. The youthful practice, still to come, of writing to the chief father figure of them all required a democratization of attitudes in the young nation as well as an expansion of schooling for young citizens. Most of Washington's letters to children were to his nieces and nephews, stepgrandchildren, and distant cousins. Outside the family, President Washington wrote to the young son of the Marquis de Lafayette. Although most of Jefferson's missives were to his grandchildren, he wrote a letter to the child of a stranger in Philadelphia (which later received an endorsement at the bottom from Andrew Jackson). Other early presidents wrote to sons and daughters as well as to a supply of wards, which reflects the early and frequent deaths of close relatives and friends. Andrew Jackson seems to have been especially encumbered by an excess of wards. The childless president loved children and oversaw the education, stormy as it sometimes was, of a large brood, including the nephew he adopted—the son of a deceased officer comrade—and a Creek boy, rejected by his tribe when he was orphaned at age three.

The practice of writing to the president on matters of youthful concern and the president's responding to such letters from young people had become a tradition even before the Civil War. A few have become famous, such as Lincoln's response to the girl who recommended that he grow a beard. It remains one of the most memorable letters ever written in America. Another anticipated a later war. In 1916, newspapers picked up a story from the *New York Tribune* that former president Theodore Roosevelt had contributed to a fund to build a battleship that a thirteen-year-old girl had begun with a dime, and printed the ever-militant TR's warm letter to the young financier Marjorie Sterrett.

Much of presidential mail to children illuminates little-known aspects of chief executives whose personalities as well as presidencies seem almost to have faded from history. Washington's advice to a nubile and sexually precocious niece, Jefferson's counsel to a grandchild on how to write a satisfactory letter, and the marginally educated Jackson's sense of deprivation at his lack of learning are aspects of larger personalities better known for their broad involvement in public affairs. The surprises are to see how a Fillmore, a Pierce, a Garfield, or a Hayes reacts to young people, and we are often happily gratified in our lesser presidents.

Many of our least-known occupants of the Oval Office show an almost unexpected humanity: The full-bearded former Civil War general Benjamin Harrison sends a doll to a four-year-old who charmed him when his train stopped briefly at a town in Indiana. The severe Tennessean James Polk is mortified at the demerits his ward receives as a West Point plebe, yet rigidly refuses to exercise any White House influence on the boy's behalf. The crusty New England Puritanism of Franklin Pierce anticipates stern Calvin Coolidge, who worries from the White House about his son's lavish $1.50 trouser pressing. The mild Millard Fillmore muses over mortality to his daughter, much as does the outwardly tough Andrew Jackson to a ward. And Lyndon Johnson in the 1960s suffuses his letters to children with as many homilies as an early nineteenth-century president.

John Kennedy once pointed out to a collection of notables in the arts and sciences invited to the White House that there was more intelligence then gathered together than at any time since Jefferson had dined there alone. It was a graceful compliment to a predecessor; yet one discovers on reading John Tyler's letters to his children that in the Tidewater Virginia lawyer-planter (and slaveowner), one of America's least-remembered presidents, Jefferson had a formidable intellectual rival.

Among other forgettable chief executives, one finds glimpses of a private integrity and charm in letters to young people that the public record seldom if ever reveals. A letter from James Garfield, whose term was cut short by assassination, cautions his sons not to gloat over his nomination to the presidency. Rutherford Hayes, amid the turmoil of his disputed election in 1876, warns his son Ruddy to be "very guarded in speech. If Mr. Tilden is elected all good citizens will quietly acquiesce, and will wish to give him and his administration fair play. If we are successful, it will not be handsome behavior for any of my family to exhibit exultation or to talk boastingly, or be vain about it."

Integrity surfaces in other ways as well, as Woodrow Wilson politely turns down requests ostensibly from children for jobs for their fathers, and William McKinley refuses to use his presidential influence to secure army commissions for his nephews. Lack of integrity at its most flagrant, however, is only hinted at in the disputed record. Nan Britton, in a controversial 1927 memoir, *The President's Daughter*, described how, beginning as a teenager, she wrote to Warren Harding, her alleged seducer, on a small lined notepad, placing her letters in a series of envelopes of graduated sizes, the innermost to be opened by Harding alone. He would respond using anonymous blue envelopes, mailed by special delivery to arrive on Sunday mornings. Britton had a daughter, Elizabeth Ann, but whether she was the president's child can only be surmised, as both sides of the claimed correspondence have disappeared. By arrangement with the protective Harding family, the Library of Congress acquired papers that must remain under seal until July 29, 2014. Even then the mystery may remain.

We want to see our presidents as large men of broad vision and as humane men of profound sensibility. They do not always live up to our hopes. John Adams, with all good will, attempts to mold his children in his dour image, and his own failings in personality make him, and his son John Quincy Adams (a man of many talents and great courage), the first two presidents unable to win the votes for a second term. James Buchanan, another one-term president, is more forthright with his wards than he is with his political rivals. William Howard Taft reveals in his letters that he is less interested in the very serious illness of his wife, which would lead most husbands to cancel a junket, than he is in the ceremonial flummeries of the presidency. And Herbert Hoover amiably and pragmatically advises a young girl, in traditional Republican Party fashion, to disburse privately the money and clothing she offers the White House to aid the Depression poor.

Even those personal letters appear in retrospect more satisfactory than the many thousands to children since Grover Cleveland's day that have been mailed from the White House but that the presidents never saw. From Cleveland's White House, an aide would brush off a child's query because the president was allegedly too busy even to append his signature to a clerk-composed form letter. For these young people, the warmth had vanished from the White House, yet the urge to make contact with the president remained. When, in 1938, the Lone Ranger on his popular radio show urged children to each send a dime to the president to help fight infantile paralysis, after Franklin D. Roosevelt, a victim of the disease, had encouraged the setting up of the National Foundation, 30,000 letters arrived the next day, 50,000 the following day, and 150,000 on the third day after the broadcast. Executive Office business nearly ceased as fifty extra postal clerks attempted to separate the official and business mail from the scrawled and smeared envelopes from children who, despite economic hard times, had parted with their dimes. With the help of Mrs Roosevelt's staff, and volunteers, it took four months before the 2,680,000 dimes were extricated and separated from other White House mail. Obviously the deluge could not have been responded to by F.D.R.—or any other president.

Most mail from children, even in less chaotic periods, was now also fielded by staff. One boy who received a brusque reply after writing to President Roosevelt apologized that he didn't know that so many people wrote to the White House "asking for something." He would wait another seven years, he promised, until prosperity returned. Yet he could not resist a postscript: "I still wish I could get a bike." Another such request arrived from a boy who wrote to Roosevelt from Cuba. It does not appear to have received even a form-letter reply. The boy was Fidel Castro. His letter is included in this book.

Most of the letters from Harry Truman's White House to youngsters dismissed serious requests as well as appeals for his autograph as an unnecessary burden upon the president's time and energy. Few letters passed the barrier of his diligent staff. One young writer began, wishing him well on his taking on the unexpected presidency upon Roosevelt's death, "Although I am only a young girl and unimportant, I am hoping that this letter will not stop at your secretary but will be read by you." It wasn't, having terminated at the desk of presidential assistant William D. Hassett, who wrote to her that the president (who never saw the letter) was "deeply touched." Hassett had been intercepting and answering presidential mail since 1935, ten years earlier.

Although Truman asked to see a broad sample of ordinary mail, he could read only what was selected for him. In the nearly twenty years after his presidency, he responded to many young people, exhorting them to study the history of their country and to learn how to be good citizens. His successor, Dwight Eisenhower, on the other hand, even as president, let himself go in writing to children. The audience via the White House mailroom was so different from that of his earlier, military experience that he enjoyed working on responses to young people, and, like Lyndon Johnson later, he had a public relations–conscious staff who understood the special value of children.

The Kennedy years were a golden age of such exchanges. John Kennedy's youth, charm, and vigor magnetized children, and many of the five thousand letters that arrived at 1600 Pennsylvania Avenue every day were from young people. Every fiftieth letter was pulled from the pile of incoming mail and sent to the Oval Office as a sampling of constituent response, but Kennedy often wandered into the mailroom and pulled additional letters from the sacks, many of them, as the handwriting on the envelopes suggested, from children. One proposed sending a man into space, rather than a dog, because "a good dog is hard to find." Another offered a photograph of himself to hang in the White House. A boy who assumed that Kennedy, as an Irishman, was an expert on Irish lore, questioned whether leprechauns were real. But the bulk of the White House responses were composed in a wooden bureaucratic prose that the chief executive never saw. The mechanical signature closely resembled Kennedy's scrawl. Those replies that he composed himself, however, are among the most delightful letters from any White House era.

The concept of a signature machine, now a commercially omnipresent device, suggests an end to the charm of an authentic message beginning, warmly, "Dear young friend . . ." Further, the advent of politically motivated letters to young people, intended by White House officials to be released to the press, also suggests a gloomy prognosis for authentic epistolary relations between presidents and children. Sometimes, however, real emotions did overtake even the most politically cynical of administrations. From the paranoically politicized Richard Nixon White House emerged the sensitive letter to young Terry Eagleton, son of George McGovern's abandoned vice presidential nominee. Nixon had not forgotten how, in the Eisenhower years, he had almost been jettisoned from the ticket himself. And Nixon's letters to the Kennedy children after their revisit to the White House, once their home, reveal an unexpected dimension to the disgraced president.

The letters, along with some of the mail that triggered them, are a striking lens through which to view our presidents as well as a way to examine the development of an increasingly more public presidency. We see the continuing—and sometimes changing—concerns of the presidential office and its occupants, and how these concerns are approached in letters to young people. Issues such as education, citizenship, and national purpose appear in tandem with personal problems, from a dog, a bike, a doll to a job or a bride. Just as we see vast changes in the nature of the presidency reflected in letters from presidents to children, to whom it was once easy to let the presidential hair down, we can also see that some things have changed little if at all since Washington. Americans have survived large men and small men in the great office, and even most of the small ones have been individuals in whom one could take some pride. The system works, and we can see it working in miniature scale here.

Rodelle Weintraub
Stanley Weintraub

Note on Texts

Wherever possible, the letters have been transcribed from the original texts, which, in many cases—those of Andrew Jackson the most obvious—differ from scrubbed-up versions published in what had been assumed to be authoritative editions. Punctuation, especially in the earlier letters, is informal and inconsistent. Some writers, for example, Franklin Pierce, rarely used a period, preferring a dash or no closing punctuation at all. In the letters up to about 1870, typical of the times, spelling of words and names is often inconsistent, idiosyncratic, and abbreviated. Their flavor has been retained.

CHAPTER ONE

The Aristocratic Presidency, 1789–1861

The presidency, from George Washington through the courtly but ineffectual James Buchanan, was essentially an aristocratic office, occupied by generals and gentleman squires. Some, like Washington, were both. Although the squirearchy from Virginia (save for the Massachusetts Adamses) dominated the office, one could also be a squire from New York (Van Buren) or Pennsylvania (Buchanan). The outsiders to the office, except for Jackson—a general and, via his Hermitage plantation, a belated squire—were men of small mark or abbreviated terms of office, accidental presidents for their times.

The aristocratic qualities of the early presidency are reflected in the letters to children from the chief executives of the first seventy years of the young nation. It seems no coincidence that the fourth and fifth presidents, Madison and Monroe, from whom no letters to young people survive, addressed their messages to Native American tribes to "My Children." The concept that the president was their Great White Father had been carefully cultivated.

Social divisions in America were still such that patronizing preliminaries were implicit, although unstated, in salutations to even more ordinary folk. But the common citizen was seldom addressed on any account. Just as the presidency was not so much a public office with a popular mandate as an aristocratic gentleman's more spacious estate—the nation—or a general's more expansive field of action, presidential letters to children, when such were written at all in the first seven decades, evidence not so much broad national consensus as concerns for the chief executive's extended family. Only here and there—as in an unusual Jefferson/Jackson letter to an obscure Philadelphia boy—do we perceive the beginnings of a democratizing of the office.

GEORGE WASHINGTON (1789–1797)
The Father of his Country had no children of his own, but he treated the offspring of his wife's earlier marriage as his family. He was particularly fond of

his stepgrandchildren and his nieces and nephews, deluging them with paternal advice. His counsel was always practical and humane rather than sophisticated and bookish, for he always felt handicapped by what he considered had been his inferior education. In the wavering practice of his time, he was inconsistent about spelling and punctuation.

Only one letter to a child included here precedes Washington's presidency. The Marquis de Lafayette had been a young man in his early twenties who left a young family behind him when he volunteered to serve the American cause. He spent years abroad while his children were growing up. Young Anastasia de Lafayette, learning English, tried it out in an appeal to Washington, who sent a response to her via her father. Later, Washington exchanged letters with Lafayette's teenage son, his namesake, George Washington Lafayette, then visiting the new nation.

Other than these letters, Washington's extant correspondence with young people addresses his acquired family. Nephews and grandsons become old enough for advanced schooling, as well as for reprimands. Nieces, granddaughters, and young cousins have adolescent problems and finally become safely marriageable. One niece, Harriet, cost Washington much in both worry and dollars. As he wrote from Mount Vernon to his sister, Betty Lewis, sending Harriet briefly to the Lewises in Fredericksburg, Harriet "comes [to you] . . . very well provided with everything proper for a girl in her situation; this much I know, that she costs me enough to place her in it. I do not however want you (or any one else) to do more by her than merely to admit her into your family whilst this House [of mine] is uninhabited by a female white woman, and therefore rendered an unfit place for her to remain at. . . . Harriet has sense enough, but no disposition to industry . . . but she is young and may yet make a fine woman."

Washington was particularly interested in the romantic problems of the younger generation. He eagerly offered his views on love and marriage to Mistress Harriet as well as to Martha's granddaughters and was relieved that, in the last year of his presidency, Harriet found a suitor, especially when Betty Lewis reported that the prospective husband was "sober, sedate, and attentive to business." After Washington left office and settled down to what he hoped would be quieter years, his days were disrupted by pleading letters from relatives, including young ones. Ever patient, the ex-president responded. Such mail continued to beset him until his death in 1799.

Anastasia Louise Pauline de Lafayette to George Washington
General Lafayette had left for home in 1781, at the successful conclusion of the revolution in America, but returned for a visit in 1784. At the time his daughter, who was seven, was beginning to learn English.

*Paris
12 June 1784*

Dear Washington,
I hope that papa whill come back so[o]n here. I am verry sorry for the loss of him, but I am verry glade for your self. I wish you a verry good health and I am with great respect, dear sir, your most obedient servant,
anastasie la fayette

George Washington to Mademoiselle de Lafayette
The letterbook copy in the Washington Papers includes no complimentary close or signature, or place from which the letter to General Lafayette's young daughter was written. It also gives the wrong date of Anastasia's letter to Washington.

November 25, 1784

To Mademoiselle de Lafayette
Permit me to thank you my dear little correspondent for the favor of her letter of the 18th. of June last, and to impress her with the idea of the pleasure I shall derive in a continuation of them. Her papa is restored to her with all the good health, paternal affection and honors her tender heart could wish.

He will carry a kiss to her from me, (which might be more agreeable from a pretty boy) and give her assurance of the affectionate regard with which I have the pleasure of being her well wisher.
[*Washington*]

George Washington to His Nephew George Steptoe Washington

*Philadelphia
December 5, 1790*

Dear George:
Agreeably to the promise which I gave to you in Virginia, I have made the necessary enquiries respecting the course of studies and expences, which

would enable you and your Brother Lawrence to finish your education at the college in this place, provided you are Masters of those books and studies, which you informed me you had passed through.

The enclosed account of studies and expences, which I wish you to return to me, you will see is under the hand of the reverend Dr. Smith Provost of the College, and may therefore be relied upon for its accuracy. After you and Lawrence have carefully perused and well considered the enclosed statement, I wish you to determine whether you will come or not. If your determination should be in favor of coming on, I must impress this upon you both in the strongest manner viz. that you come with good dispositions and full resolutions to pursue your studies closely, conform to the established rules and customs of the College, and to conduct yourselves on all occasions with decency and propriety.

To you, George, I would more particularly address myself at this time, as from your advanced age it may be presumed that such advice, as I am about to give will make a deeper impression upon you than upon your Brother, and your conduct may very probably mark the line of his; But, at the same time Lawrence must remember that this is equally applicable to him.

Should you enter upon the course of studies here marked out you must consider it as the finishing of your education, and, therefore, as the time is limited, that every hour misspent is lost for ever, and that future *years* cannot compensate for lost *days* at this period of your life. This reflection must shew the necessity of an unremitting application to your studies. To point out the importance of circumspection in your conduct, it may be proper to observe that a good moral character is the first essential in a man, and that the habits contracted here may stamp your character through life. It is therefore highly important that you should endeavor not only to be learned but virtuous. Much more might be said to shew the necessity of application and regularity, but when you must know that without them you can never be qualfied to render service to your country, assistance to your friends, or consolidation to your retired moments, nothing further need be said to prove their utility.

As to your clothing, it will, I presume, cost much the same here as in Alexandria. I shall always wish to see you clothed decently and becoming your stations; but I shall ever discountenance extravagance or foppishness in your dress. At all times, and upon all occasions I shall be happy to give you both such marks of my approbation, as your progress and good conduct merit.

If you determine to come on, you had better do it immediately, and Major Washington will furnish you with such money as may be necessary for the Stage and expences from Alexandria to this place. But I must repeat what

I have before enjoined, that you come with good dispositions and determined resolutions to conform to establishments and pursue your studies.

Your aunt joins me in love to you both, and best wishes to Dr. Craik and family. I am, dear George, your sincere friend and affectionate uncle.

G. Washington

George Washington to Mistress Harriet Washington
Harriet, whose name her anxious uncle misspelled, was the daughter of his late brother, Samuel, and both nubile and naughty.

*Philadelphia
October 30, 1791*

Dear Harriot:

I have received your letter of the 21st. instant, and shall always be glad to hear from you. When my business will permit inclination it will not be wanting in me to acknowledge the receipt of your letters, and this I shall do more cheerfully as it will afford me opportunities at those times of giving you such occasional advice, as your situation may require.

At present I could plead a better excuse for curtailing my letter to you than you had for shortening of yours to me, having a multitude of business before me while you have nothing to do, consequently you might, with equal convenience to yourself, have set down to write your letter an hour or two, or even a day sooner, as to have delayed it until your Cousin was on the point of sending to the Post-Office. I make this remark for no other reason than to shew you it is better to offer no excuse than a bad one, if at any time you should happen to fall into an error.

Occupied as my time now is, and must be during the sitting of Congress, I nevertheless will endeavor to inculcate upon your mind the delicacy and danger of that period, to which you are now arrived under peculiar circumstances. You are just entering into the state of womanhood, without the watchful eye of a Mother to admonish, or the protecting aid of a Father to advise and defend you; you may not be sensible that you are at this moment about to be stamped with that character which will adhere to you through life; the consequence of which you have not perhaps attended to, but be assured it is of the utmost importance that you should.

Your cousins, with whom you live are well qualified to give you advice, and I am sure they will if you are disposed to receive it. But if you are disobliging, self-willed, and untowardly it is hardly to be expected that they will engage themselves in unpleasant disputes with you, especially Fanny, whose mild and placid temper will not permit her to exceed the limits of wholesome admonition or gentle rebuke. Think then to what dangers a giddy girl of 15 or 16 must be exposed in circumstances like these. To be under but little or no controul may be pleasing to a mind that does not reflect, but this pleasure cannot be of long duration, and reason, too late perhaps, may convince you of the folly of mis-spending time. You are now to learn, I am certain, that your fortune is small; supply the want of it then with a well cultivated mind; with dispositions to industry and frugality; with gentleness of manners, obliging temper, and such qualifications as will attract notice, and recommend you to a happy establishment for life.

You might instead of associating with those from whom you can derive nothing that is good, but may have observed every thing that is deceitful, lying, and bad, become the intimate companion of and aid to your Cousin in the domestic concerns of the family. Many Girls before they have arrived at your age have been found so trustworthy as to take the whole trouble of a family from their Mothers; but it is by a steady and rigid attention to the rules of propriety that such confidence is obtained, and nothing would give me more pleasure than to hear that you had acquired it. The merits and benefits of it would redound more to your advantage in your progress thro' life, and to the person with whom you may in due time form a matrimonial connexion than to any others; but to none would such a circumstance afford more real satisfaction, than to Your affectionate Uncle.

G. Washington

George Washington to George Washington Lafayette

The marquis's son appeared in Boston late in 1795, accompanied by a tutor and determined to study in the United States. Washington wanted to greet the boy but worried that seeing him might endanger the precarious neutrality the nation was attempting to maintain between France and England. Still, he made sure that the boy was well cared for in Boston. Finally, two months later, Washington decided that it was now safe to communicate with young Lafayette.

Philadelphia
November 22, 1795

My dear young friend:

It was with sincere pleasure I recieved your letter from Boston, and with the heart of affection I welcome you to this Ctry.

Considerations of a political nature added to those which were assigned by yourself, or Mr. Frestal of a sort more private, but not less interesting to your friends left no doubt in my mind of the propriety of your remaining incog until some plan advantageous to *yourself* and eligible for *all* parties could be devised for bringing you forwd. under more favorable auspices.

These considerations, and a journey which I was in the act of commencing when I received your letter (and from which I have not long since been returned to this city) restrained me from writing to you at that time, but I imposed upon Mr. Cabot a gentleman of character and one in whose discretion I could place entire confidence, the agreeable office of assuring you, in my name, of my warmest affection and support; of my determination to stand in the place of a father and friend to you undr. all cirs; requesting him at the same time to make arrangemts. with Mr. Frestal for supplying your immediate wants, and moreover that he would add thereto every thing consolatory on my part. All of which I now renew to you in the most unequivocal terms; for you may be assured, that the sincere, and affectionate attachment which I had to your unfortunate father, my friend and compatriot in arms will extend with not less warmth to you, his son; do not therefore ascribe my silence from the period of your interview with Mr. Cabot to a wrong cause.

The causes, which have imposed this conduct on us both, not being entirely removed, it is my desire, that you, and Mr. Frestal would repair to Colo. Hamilton, in the City of New York, who is authorised by me to fix with you on the most eligible plan for your present accommodation. This gentleman was always in habits of great intimacy with, and is warmly attached to, Mr. de la Fayette; you may rely therefore on his friendship and the efficacy of his advice.

How long the causes wch. have withheld you from me may continue, I am not able, at this moment to decide but be assured of my wishes to embrace you so soon as they shall have ceased and that whenever the period arrives I shall do it with fervency. In the meantime let me begin with fatherly advice to you to apply closely to your studies that the season of your youth may be improved to the utmost; that you may be found the deserving Son of a meritorious father. Adieu; believe me to be as you will always find me Your Affecte. friend

G. Washington

George Washingto to Eleanor Parke Custis
Nellie Custis was growing into a beautiful young teenager when Washington wrote his stepgranddaughter to be wary of the very charms she knew she possessed.

Philadelphia
January 16, 1795

Dear Nellie:

Your letter, the receipt of which I am now acknowledging, is written correctly and in fair characters, which is an evidence that you command, when you please, a fair hand. Possessed of these advantages, it will be your own fault if you do not avail yourself of them, and attention being paid to the choice of your subjects, you can have nothing to fear from the malignancy of criticism, as your ideas are lively, and your descriptions agreeable. Let me touch a little now on your Georgetown ball, and happy, thrice happy, for the fair who were assembled on the occasion, that there was a man to spare; for had there been 79 ladies and only 78 gentlemen, there might, in the course of the evening, have been some disorder among the caps; notwithstanding the apathy which *one* of the company entertains for the "*youth*" of the present day, and her determination "never to give herself a moment's uneasiness on account of any of them." A hint here: men and women feel the same inclinations to each other *now* that they always have done, and which they will continue to do until there is a new order of things, and *you,* as others have done, may find, perhaps, that the passions of your sex are easier raised than allayed. Do not therefore boast too soon or too strongly of your insensibility to, or resistance of, its powers. In the composition of the human frame there is a good deal of inflammable matter, however dormant it may lie for a time, and like an intimate acquaintance of yours, when the torch is put to it, *that* which is *within you* may burst into a blaze; for which reason and especially too, as I have entered upon the chapter of advices, I will read you a lecture drawn from this text.

Love is said to be an involuntary passion, and it is, therefore, contended that it cannot be resisted. This is true in part only, for like all things else, when nourished and supplied plentifully with aliment, it is rapid in its progress; but let these be withdrawn and it may be stifled in its birth or much stinted in its growth. For example, a woman (the same may be said of the other sex) all beautiful and accomplished, will, while her hand and heart are undisposed of, turn the heads and set the circle in which she moves on fire. Let her marry, and what is the consequence? The madness *ceases* and all is quiet again. Why? not because there is any diminution in the charms of the lady, but because there is an end of hope. Hence it follows, that love may and therefore ought to be under the guidance of reason, for although we cannot avoid first impressions, we may assuredly place them under guard; and my motives for treating on this subject are to show you, while you remain Eleanor Parke Custis, spinster, and retain the resolution to love with moderation, the propriety of adhering to the latter resolution, at least until you have secured your game, and the way by which it may be accomplished.

When the fire is beginning to kindle, and your heart growing warm, propound these questions to it. Who is this invader? Have I a competent knowledge of him? Is he a man of good character; a man of sense? For, be assured, a sensible woman can never be happy with a fool. What has been his walk in life? Is he a gambler, a spendthrift, or drunkard? Is his fortune sufficient to maintain me in the manner I have been accustomed to live, and my sisters do live, and is he one to whom my friends can have no reasonable objection? If these interrogatories can be satisfactorily answered, there will remain but one more to be asked, that, however, is an important one. Have I sufficient ground to conclude that his affections are engaged by me? Without this the heart of sensibility will struggle against a passion that is not reciprocated; delicacy, custom, or call it by what epithet you will, having precluded all advances on your part. The declaration, without the *most direct* invitation of yours, must proceed from the man, to render it permanent and valuable, and nothing short of good sense and an easy unaffected conduct can draw the line between prudery and coquetry. It would be no great departure from truth to say, that it rarely happens otherwise than that a thorough-paced coquette dies in celibacy, as a punishment for her attempts to mislead others, by encouraging looks, words, or actions, given for no other purpose than to draw men on to make overtures that they may be rejected.

This day, according to our information, gives a husband to your elder sister, and consummates, it is to be presumed, her fondest desires. The dawn with us is bright, and propitious, I hope, of her future happiness, for a full measure of which she and Mr. Law have my earnest wishes. Compliments and congratulations on this occasion, and best regards are presented to your mamma, Dr. Stuart and family; and every blessing, among which a good husband when you want and deserve one, is bestowed on you by yours, affectionately.

G. Washington

George Washington to Mistress Sally Ball Haynie
Mistress Haynie was a young cousin on Washington's mother's side of the family. She had apparently been employed as a companion or governess.

Mount Vernon
February 11, 1798

Miss Salley:

I have received your letter of the 28th. of last month, and without enquiry at this time why you left Mr. Lewis's family or how you employ your time, I have requested him to furnish you with ten pounds to supply you with such necessaries as you may be in immediate want.

But as you have no fortune to support you, Industry, oeconomy, and a virtuous conduct are your surest resort, and best dependance. In every station of life, these are commendable. In the one in which it has pleased Providence to place you, it is indispensably necessary that they should mark all your footsteps. It is no disparagement to the first lady in the Land to be constantly employed, at some work or another; to you, it would prove, in addition to a chaste and unsullied reputation the surest means of attracting the notice of some man with whom your future fortune will be united in a Matrimonial bond and without which it would be in vain to expect a person of worth. I wish you well and am Your friend.

G. Washington

JOHN ADAMS (1797–1801)

Family austerity and ambition are reflected early in John Adams's crustily affectionate letters to his son John Quincy (b. 1767) and to his daughter Abigail (b. 1765) as well as later to his grandchildren. Seldom in his beloved Braintree, Massachusetts, after the start of the rebellion, Adams served his country from afar, first in a mission to France, then as a minister to negotiate treaties of peace and commerce with Great Britain, and then on a mission to the Netherlands, where he first placed his sons Charles (b. 1770) and John Quincy in a Latin school at Amsterdam. As he traveled, his chief contacts with his children had been by letters, but his contacts grew more attenuated when John Quincy, just fourteen in July 1881 but already accomplished in languages, left his studies in Holland for St. Petersburg to become secretary to Francis Dana, who had been appointed American minister to Russia. John Adams was often apart, too, from both Abigails, his wife and his daughter. Except when the family was all too briefly reunited, the letters from one Adams to another were numerous, and carefully preserved in their originals and in copies in letterbooks. Yet Abigail once complained in a letter to her husband about John Quincy, "Do you know I have not a line from him for a year and a half. —Alass my dear I am much afflicted with a disorder call'd the *Heart-ach,* nor can any remedy be found in America."

The Adams letterbooks for the period of the presidency contain no letters to young people outside the family. There was as yet no tradition for that. Adams was a New Englander of unrelenting principles, and it is unlikely that anything he wrote earlier to young Abigail or John Quincy would have been enunciated any less rigorously or differently to lesser folk, or moderated from his vantage point as chief executive.

Late in life, the former president mellowed just enough to write to his grandson, John Adams Smith, during the War of 1812, about the ineffectiveness of the pygmy American Navy, that it was "so lilliputian that Hercules after a hasty dinner would sink it by setting his foot on it. I had like to say that Gulliver might bury it in the deep by making water on it." Smith might have been Adams's *"Cher petit fils,"* but Adams never would have written in that scatological Swiftian way to a child.

Apparently Adams's interest in the navy was a public matter, for as late as 1821 a youth "as unknown to me as any stripling in the moon" wrote to him to ask his help in getting to sea. The former president sent the inquiry to the Secretary of the Navy, adding, "Who knows but that this child may be destined to be another [Oliver Hazard] Perry." No letter to the boy himself appears to have survived.

John Adams to His Son John Quincy Adams

Although young John Quincy was at the University of Leyden, in the Netherlands, he was only thirteen.

Amsterdam Decr. 20. 1780

My Son

You are now at an University, where many of the greatest Men have received their Education.

Many of the most famous Characters, which England has produced, have pursued their Studies for some time at Leyden. Some, tho not many of the Sons of America, have studied there.

I would have you attend all the Lectures in which Experiments are made whether in Philosophy, Medicine or Chimistry, because these will open your mind for Inquiries into Nature: but by no means neglect the Languages.

I wish you to write me, an Account of all the Professorships, and the names of the Professors. I should also be obliged to you for as good an Account of the Constitution of the University as you can obtain. Let me know what degrees are conferred there; by whom; and what Examination the Candidates undergo, in order to be admitted to them.

I am your affectionate Father,

John Adams

John Adams to His Son John Quincy Adams

Amsterdam Dec. 28. 1780

My Son

The Ice is so universal now that I suppose you spend some Time in Skaiting every day. it is a fine Exercise for young Persons, and therefore I am willing to indulge you in it, provided you confine yourself to proper Hours, and to strict Moderation. Skaiting is a fine Art. It is not Simple Velocity or Agility that constitutes the Perfection of it but Grace. There is an Elegance of Motion, which is charming to the sight, and is useful to acquire, because it obliges you to restrain that impetuous Ardour and violent Activity, into which the Agitation of Spirits occasioned by this Exercise is apt to hurry you, and which is inconsistent both with your Health and Pleasure.

At Leyden, I suppose you may see many Gentlemen, who are perfect in the Art.—I have walked, several Times round this City from the Gate of Utrecht to that of Harlem, and seen some thousands Skaiting upon the Cingel, since the Frost set in. I have seen many skait with great Spirit, some with prodigious Swiftness, a few with a tolerably genteel Air, but none with that inimitable Grace and Beauty which I have seen some Examples of, in other Countries, even in our own.

I have seen some Officers of the British Army, at Boston, and some of our Army at Cambridge, skait with as perfect Elegance, as if they had spent their whole Lives in the study of Hogarths Principles of Beauty, and in reducing them to Practice.

I would advise you, my Son, in Skaiting, Dancing and Riding, to be always attentive to this Grace, which is founded in natural Principles, and is therefore as much for your Ease and Use, as for your Pleasure.

Do not conclude from this, that I advise you to spend much of your Time or Thoughts upon these Exercises and Diversions. In Truth I care very little about any of them. They should never be taken but as Exercise and Relaxation of Business and study. But as your Constitution requires vigorous Exercise, it will not be amiss, to spend some of your Time, in swimming, Riding, Dancing, Fencing and Skaiting, which are all manly Amusements, and it is as easy to learn by a little Attention, to perform them all with Taste, as it is to execute them in a slovenly, Awkward and ridiculous Manner.

Every Thing in Life should be done with Reflection, and Judgment, even the most insignificant Amusements. They should all be arranged in subordination, to the great Plan of Happiness, and Utility. That you may attend early to this Maxim is the Wish of your affectionate Father,

John Adams

John Quincy Adams to His Father John Adams

St. Petersbourg October 12/23 1781

Honoured Sir

I wrote you just after I arrived here, and gave you a short sketch of my Journey from Amsterdam to this Place, and promised you in my next a description of this city, but I dont find any thing more than what Voltaire says of it in his history of Russia nor even quite so much, for according to his description, the city is situated upon the Gulf of Cronstadt in the midst of nine branches of rivers, which divide its different quarters. Seven of these nine branches of rivers are nothing more than creeks made into canals about as wide as the cingel at Amsterdam, the rest of his description is pretty exact.

I left at Amsterdam Littleton's Latin and English Dictionary which Dr. Waterhouse gave me; if I should stay here, I should be glad if you would send it to me by the first vessel that shall come here in the spring, as I can't get here any good dictionary either French and Latin or English and Latin. Indeed this is not a very good place for learning the Latin and Greek Languages, as there is no academy or school here, and but very few private teachers who demand at the rate of 90 pounds Sterling a year, for an hour and a half each day. Mr. Dana don't chuse to employ any at that extravagant price without your positive orders, but I hope I shall be able to go on alone.

The night before last it froze hard; and yesterday it snow'd a little for the first time. It snows at present; by this you see how soon the winter begins with us here, we dont find as yet that it is colder than it is sometimes in America at this time.

I am your dutiful Son,

John Q. Adams

John Adams to His Son John Quincy Adams

Amsterdam Decr. 15. 1781

My dear Child

This day Mr. Sayre arrived, with your Letter of the 12/23 of October. Yours of August I answered, Yesterday.

You have not informed me whether the Houses are built of Brick, Stone or Wood. Whether they are seven stories high or only one. How they are glazed, whether they have chimneys as in Spain. What publick Buildings, what Maison de Ville or state house. What Churches? What Palaces? What Statuary, what Paintings, Musick, Spectacles, &c. You have said nothing of the Religion of the Country, whether it is Catholick or Protestant. What is the national Church. Whether there are many Sectaries. Whether there is a Toleration of various Religions &c.

I think the Price for a Master is intolerable. If there is no Academy, nor School, nor a Master to be had, I really dont know what to say to your staying in Russia. You had better be at Leyden where you might be in a regular course of Education. You might come in the Spring in a Russian, Sweedish or Prussian Vessel, to Embden perhaps or Hamborough, and from thence here, in a neutral Bottom still. I am afraid of your being too troublesome to Mr. D[ana].

However, I rely upon it that you follow your Studies with your wonted Assiduity. It is strange if no Dictionary can be found in French nor English.

I dont perceive that you take Pains enough with your Hand Writing. Believe me, from Experience, if you now in your Youth resolutely conquer your impatience, and resolve never to write the most familiar Letter or trifling Card, with[out] Attention and care, it will save you a vast deal of Time and Trouble too, every day of your whole Life. When the habit is got, it is easier to write well than ill, but this Habit is only to be acquired, in early life.

God bless my dear Son, and preserve his Health and his Manners, from the numberless dangers, that surround Us, wherever We go in this World. So prays your affectionate Father,

J. Adams

John Adams to His Daughter Abigail

The Hague, September 26, 1782

My dear Daughter

I have received your charming letter, which you forgot to date, by Mrs. Rogers. Your proposal of coming to Europe to keep your papa's house and take care of his health, is in a high strain of filial duty and affection, and the idea pleases me much in speculation, but not at all in practice. I have too much tenderness for your, my dear child, to permit you to cross the Atlantic. You know not what it is. If God shall spare me and your brother to return home, which I hope will be next Spring, I never desire to know of any of my family crossing the seas again.

I am glad you have received a small present. You ask for another; and although it would be painful for me to decline the gratification of your inclination, I must confess, I should have been happier if you had asked me for Bell's British Poets. There is more elegance and beauty, more sparkling lustre to my eyes, in one of those volumes, than in all the diamonds which I ever saw about the Princess of Orange, or the Queen of France, in all their birthday splendour.

I have a similar request under consideration, from your brother at P[etersburg]. I don't refuse either, but I must take it *ad referendum,* and deliberate upon it as long as their H[igh] M[ightiness] do upon my propositions. I have learned caution from them, and you and your brother must learn patience from me.

If you have yet so exalted sentiments of the public good as have others more advanced in life, you must endeavour to obtain them. They are the primary and most essential branch of general benevolence, and therefore the highest honour and happiness both of men and Christians, and the indispensable duty of both. Malevolence, my dear child, is its own punishment, even in this world. Indifference to the happiness of others must arise from insensibility of heart, or from a selfishness still more contemptible, or rather detestable. But for the same reason that our own individual happiness should not be our only object, that of our relatives, however near or remote, should not; but we should extend our views to as large a circle as our circumstances of birth, fortune, education, rank, and influence extend, in order to do as much good to our fellow men as we can.

You will easily see, my dear child, that jewels and lace can go but a very little way in this career. Knowledge in the head and virtue in the heart, time devoted to study or business, instead of show and pleasure, are the way to be useful and consequently happy.

Your happiness is very near to me. But depend upon it, it is simplicity, not refinement nor elegance [that] can obtain it. By conquering your taste, (for taste is to be conquered, like unruly appetites and passions, or the mind is undone,) you will save yourself many perplexities and mortifications. There are more thorns sown in the path of human life by vanity, than by any other thing.

I know your disposition to be thoughtful and serene, and therefore I am not apprehensive of your erring much in this way. Yet no body can be guarded too much against it, or too early.

Overwhelmed as I have been ever since you was born, with cares such as seldom fall to the lot of any man, I have not been able to attend to the fortunes of my family. They have no resource but in absolute frugality and incessant industry, which are not only my advice, but my injunctions upon every one of them.

With inexpressible tenderness of heart, I am Your affectionate father,
John Adams

John Adams to His Son John Quincy Adams

Paris May 14. 1783

My dear Child

Mr. Hardouin has just now called upon me, and delivered me your Letter of the 6 Instant.

I find that, although, your hand Writing is distinct and legible, yet it has not engaged so much of your Attention as to be remarkably neat. I should advise you to be very careful of it: never to write in a hurry, and never to let a slovenly Word or Letter go from you. If one begins at your Age, it is easier to learn to write well than ill, both in Characters and Style. There are not two prettier accomplishments than a handsome hand and Style, and these are only to be acquired in youth. I have suffered much, through my whole Life, from a Negligence of these Things in my young days, and I wish you to know it. Your hand and Style, are clear enough to shew that you may easily make them manly and beautifull, and when a habit is got, all is easy.

I see your Travells have been expensive, as I expected they would be: but I hope your Improvements have been worth the Money. Have you kept a regular Journal? If you have not, you will be likely to forget most of the

Observations you have made. If you have omitted this Usefull Exercise, let me advise you to recommence it, immediately. Let it be your Amusement, to minute every day, whatever you may have seen or heard worth Notice. One contracts a Fondness of Writing by Use. We learn to write readily, and what is of more importance, We think, and improve our Judgments, by committing our Thoughts to Paper.

Your Exercises in Latin and Greek must not be omitted a single day, and you should turn your Mind a little to Mathematicks. There is among my Books a Fennings Algebra. Begin it immediately and go through it, by a small Portion every day. You will find it as entertaining as an Arabean Tale. The Vulgar Fractions with which it begins, is the best extant, and you should make yourself quite familiar with it.

A regular Distribution of your Time, is of great Importance. You must measure out your Hours, for Study, Meals, Amusements, Exercise and Sleep, and suffer nothing to divert you, at least from those devoted to study.

But above all Things, my Son, take Care of your Behaviour and preserve the Character you have acquired, for Prudence and Solidity. Remember your tender Years and treat all the World with Modesty, Decency and Respect.

The Advantage you have in Mr. Dumas's Attention to you is a very prescious one. He is himself a Walking Library, and so great a Master of Languages ancient and modern is very rarely seen. The Art of asking Questions is the most essential to one who wants to learn. Never be too wise to ask a Question.

Be as frugal as possible, in your Expences.

Write to your Mamma, Sister and Brothers, as often as you have Opportunity. It will be a Grief to me to loose a Spring Passage home, but although I have my fears I dont yet despair.

Every Body gives me a very flattering Character of your Sister, and I am well pleased with what I hear of you: The principal Satisfaction I can expect in Life, in future, will be in your good Behaviour and that of my other Children. My Hopes from all of you are very agreable. God grant, I may not be dissappointed.

Your affectionate Father,

John Adams

John Adams to His Daughter Abigail

Paris, August 13th, 1783

My dear Daughter

I have received your affectionate letter of the 10th of May, with great pleasure, and another from your mother of the 28th and 29th of April, which by mistake I omitted to mention in my letter to her to-day. Your education and your welfare, my dear child, are very near to my heart; and nothing in this life would contribute so much to my happiness, next to the company of your mother, as yours. I have reason to say this by the experience I have had of the society of your brother, whom I brought with me from the Hague. He has grown to be a man, and the world says they shoud take him for my younger brother, if they did not know him to be my son. I have great satisfaction in his behaviour, as well as in the improvements he has made in his travels, and the reputation he has left behind him wherever he has been. He is very studious and delights in nothing but books, which alarms me for his health; because, like me, he is naturally inclined to be fat. His knowledge and his judgment are so far beyond his years, as to be admired by all who have conversed with him. I lament, however, that he could not have his education at Harvard College, where his brothers shall have theirs, if Providence shall afford me the means of supporting the expense of it. If my superiors shall permit me to come home, I hope it will be soon; if they mean I should stay abroad, I am not able to say what I shall do, until I know in what capacity. One thing is certain, that I will not live long without my family, and another is equally so, that I can never consent to see my wife and children croaking with me like frogs in the Fens of Holland, and burning and shivering alternately with fevers, as Mr. Tha[xt]er, Charles, Stephen[s], and myself have done: your brother John alone had the happiness to escape, but I was afraid to trust him long amidst those pestilential streams.

You have reason to wish for a taste of history, which is as entertaining and instructive to the female as to the male sex. My advice to you would be to read the history of your own country, which although it may not afford so splendid objects as some others, before the commencement of the late war, yet since that period, it is the most interesting chapter in the history of the world, and before that period is intensely affecting to every native American. You will find among your own ancestors, by your mother's side at least, characters which deserve your attention. It is by the female world, that the greatest and best characters among men are formed. I have long been of this opinion to such a degree, that when I hear of an extraordinary man, good or bad, I naturally, or habitually inquire who was his mother? There can be nothing in life more honourable for a woman, than to contribute by her virtues, her advice, her example, or her address, to the formation of an husband, a brother, or a son, to be useful to the world.

Heaven has blessed you, my daughter, with an understanding and a consideration, that is not found every day among young women, and with a mother who is an ornament to her sex. You will take care that you preserve your own character, and that you persevere in a course of conduct, worthy of the example that is every day before you. With the most fervent wishes for your happiness, I am your affectionate father,

John Adams

John Adams to His Grandson George Washington Adams
The elderly and increasingly lonely former president doted on his first grandson, fifteen at the time of this worried letter.

Quincy[, Massachusetts]
June 16th, 1816

My dear George,

You cannot easily imagine, how much Grief the news of your Indisposition has given Us. Our most chearing hopes are built upon your Foundation. Give your closest Attention to your health, for on that every Thing depends. You must study Physick; not to practise but to be your own Physician. Pray your Father to buy Dr Theynes Works, on my account. Neglected, despised and forgotten as he is, I owe my Longevity to him. Nevertheless, he must be read with caution like all other Writers and his Advice followed with Judgment and discrimination.

I agree with your amiable young Friend Claudius Bradford in his Opinion that Nature designed You for the Senate rather than the Field, and that you will be more at home in the Cabinet than in the Camp. Your Parents have given you a great Name, that may mislead you from your natural destination or rather Vocation. I know that Gratitude, not Ambition dictated your Christian Name. But have a care that you do not make it an Object of your Idolatry. We are pretty well, give my Love to Parents and Brothers and Cousin.

A.

P.S. Do you remember The Reverend Mr. William Clark who was deaf and almost dumb. His Effects have been lately Sold among which were four

Bushells of English and American Newspapers during our Revolution. They went off for Waste Paper at a dollar a Bushell. How attentive our Countrymen are to their own History? I never knew nor Suspected the Auction till it was past. An abundance of curious Documents! As I am informed.

A.

THOMAS JEFFERSON (1801–1809)

Thomas Jefferson's letters to his children began when he was at Annapolis in 1783 during the temporary exile of Congress from Philadelphia. The recently widowed father regretted being in the position of absent parent and took seriously his responsibilities toward his daughters. He concerned himself with selecting their clothing and gave careful consideration (by post) to the most trifling as well as serious questions, overwhelming them with parental advice and admonitions. Eleven-year-old Patsy (Martha) may have found his letters difficult to understand; all of them were beyond the comprehension of five-year-old Mary and the baby Lucy, whose mother had died of complications following childbirth, a not uncommon event in those days.

When Jefferson became minister to France in 1784, Martha accompanied him while Mary and Lucy remained with their mother's half sister Elizabeth Eppes and her family. After Lucy died of whooping cough at three, Jefferson sent for Mary, who wrote to him, "I don't want to go to France. I had rather stay with Aunt Eppes." Jefferson reunited what was left of his household anyway, and his relationship with Mary, who hardly knew him, remained strained. Years later, she married her aunt's eldest son, John Wayles Eppes, and left Monticello. After her early death in childbirth at twenty-six, Jefferson became close to her surviving child, Francis, writing to him regularly, remaining interested in his education, and bequeathing land to him.

One of the few letters written by an early president to a child not his own or with close familial ties is a message from Jefferson to young Thomas Jefferson Grotjan of Philadelphia, included here. Jefferson's primary correspondence with children during his presidential years, however, was not with youthful future constituents, but with his many Randolph grandchildren. Nine of the surviving eleven children of Martha and Thomas Mann Randolph, Jr., were born during or prior to Jefferson's presidency. He wanted those who were old enough to take pen in hand to write to him by every weekly post, and they all kept accounts as to letters owed. Eventually he asked Anne and Ellen Randolph to write instead on alternate weeks, explaining that it "was not that I did not wish to hear from you both oftener, but that I could not probably find time to answer more than one letter a week." He tried to return a letter every week and almost always sent some gift along with his letter: six geese, a pair of Bantam chickens, roots to plant at Monticello, "some tussocks of a grass of a perfume equal to Vanilla, called Sweet-scented Vernal grass," pens, books, and poems of his own. The children who could write reciprocated. Anne sent him some white violets, writing "I enclose [them] but fear they will lose their smell before they reach you."

Kept in Washington, away from his beloved Monticello, where his grandchildren were, Jefferson worried about the affairs of the family. He had already lost children and grandchildren, and he needed the reassurances the weekly letters brought. His involvement with, and concern for, his grandchildren remained intense all his life. He was upset when Francis Eppes married at twenty-one, worrying that the consequences of an early marriage were "the interruption of studies and the filling our houses with children." He paid for the food, clothing, and education of the Randolph children even when his own finances were straitened. In his will, he left the bulk of his estate in trust for Martha and her children so that Randolph's creditors could not claim the inheritance.

Thomas Jefferson to His Daugher Martha
Jefferson had left Martha in Philadelphia in the care of Mrs. Thomas Hopkinson, mother of his friend Francis Hopkinson, a signer of the Declaration of Independence.

Annapolis
Nov. 28, 1783

My dear Patsy

After four days journey I arrived here without any accident and in as good health as when I left Philadelphia. The conviction that you would be more improved in the situation I have placed you than if still with me, has solaced me on my parting with you, which my love for you has rendered a difficult thing. The acquirements which I hope you will make under the tutors I have provided for you will render you more worthy of my love, and if they cannot increase it they will prevent it's diminution. Consider the good lady who has taken you under her roof, who has undertaken to see that you perform all your exercises, and to admonish you in all those wanderings from what is right or what is clever to which your inexperience would expose you, consider her I say as your mother, as the only person to whom, since the loss with which heaven has been pleased to afflict you, you can now look up; and that here displeasure or disapprobation on any occasion will be an immense misfortune which should you be so unhappy as to incur by any unguarded act, think no concession too much to regain her good will. With respect to the distribution of your time the following is what I should approve.

from 8. to 10 o'clock practise music.

from 10. to 1. dance one day and draw another

from 1. to 2. draw on the day you dance, and write a letter the next day.

from 3. to 4. read French.

from 4. to 5. exercise yourself in music.

from 5. till bedtime read English, write &c.

Communicate this plan to Mrs. Hopkinson and if she approves of it pursue it. As long as Mrs. Trist remains in Philadelphia cultivate her affections. She has been a valuable friend to you and her good sense and good heart make her valued by all who know her and by nobody on earth more than by me. I expect you will write to me by every post. Inform me what books you read, what tunes you learn, and inclose me your best copy of every lesson in drawing. Write also one letter every week either to your aunt Eppes, your aunt Skipwith, your aunt Carr, or the little lady from whom I now inclose a letter, and always put the letter you so write under cover to me. Take care that you never spell a word wrong. Always before you write a word consider how it is spelt, and if you do not remember it, turn to a dictionary. It produces great praise to a lady to spell well. I have placed my happiness on seeing you good and accomplished, and no distress which this world can now bring on me could equal that of your disappointing my hopes. If you love me then, strive to be good under every situation and to all living creatures, and to acquire those accomplishments which I have put in your power, and which will go far towards ensuring you the warmest love of your affectionate father,

Th: Jefferson

P.S. Keep my letters and read them at times that you may always have present in your mind those things which will endear you to me.

Thomas Jefferson to His Grandchildren Anne Cary Randolph, Thomas Jefferson Randolph, and Ellen Wayles Randolph

Washington
Mar. 2. 1802.

My dear children

I am very happy to find that two of you can write. I shall now expect that whenever it is inconvenient for your papa and mama to write, one of you will write on a piece of paper these words 'all is well' and send it for me to the post office: I am happy too that Miss Ellen can now read so readily. If she will make haste and read through all the books I have given her, and will let me know when she is through them, I will go and carry her some more. I shall now see whether she wishes to see me as much as she says. I wish to see you all: and the more I perceive that you are all advancing in your learning and improving in good dispositions the more I shall love you, and the more every body will love you. It is a charming thing to be loved by every body: and the way to obtain it is, never to quarrel or be angry with any body and to tell a story. Do all the kind things you can to your companions, give them every thing rather than to yourself. Pity and help any thing you see in distress and learn your books and improve your minds. This will make every body fond of you, and desirous of doing it to you. Go on then my dear children, and, when we meet at Monticello, let me see who has improved most. I kiss this paper for each of you: it will therefore deliver the kisses to yourselves, and two over, which one of you must deliver to your Mama for me; and present my affectionate attachment to your papa. Yourselves love and Adieux.

TH: JEFFERSON

Thomas Jefferson to His Granddaughter Ellen Wayles Randolph

Washington
May 21. 05.

MISS ELEANOR W. RANDOLPH TO TH: JEFFERSON	DR.
1805. May 21. To a letter which ought to be written once in every 3. weeks, while I am here, to wit from Jan. 1. 1805. to this day 15. weeks	5.
CR.	

Feb. 23. By one single letter of this day's date	1
Balance due from E. W. Randolph to Th: J Letters	4
	5

So stands the account for this year, my dear Ellen, between you and me. Unless it be soon paid off, I shall send the sheriff after you. I inclose you an abundant supply of poetry, among which you will find Goody Blake,* which I think you wanted. I will thank you if you will put on your boots and spurs and ride to Monticello and inform me how my thorns live. This part of the country is beautifying with them so fast that every ride I take makes me anxious for those at Monticello. Your Papa in his last letter informs me that mumps have got into the family. Let me know who have it and how all do. Kiss your dear Mama for me and shake hands with all the little ones. Present me affectionately to your Papa and accept mes baise-mains yourself.

TH: JEFFERSON

Thomas Jefferson to His Granddaughter Ellen Wayles Randolph

Washington
Mar. 1. 07.

My dearest Ellen

I am afraid I shall be bankrupt in my epistolary account with Anne and yourself. However the tide of business, like that of the ocean, will wait for nobody. I send for Cornelia a little poem, the grasshopper's ball,† to begin her collection. The Yankee story is for yourself. Thank Mary for her letter, but tell her it is written in a cypher of which I have not the key. She must therefore tell it all to me when I come home. I shall write to Anne by the cart, because it will carry a box of flower roots which I shall consign to her care, but not to be opened till we get to Monticello, and have every thing

---

*"Goody Blake and Harry Gill" is a poem by William Wordsworth published in his *Lyrical Ballads* (1798), about a poor old women caught by the well-to-do Harry Gill while stealing wood for a fire from his hedge. Kneeling on the sticks she prays, "O may he never more be warm!" He then shivers his life away, no matter how much he dons for warmth—a lesson in sensitivity and tolerance which Jefferson proposes to his granddaughter.

†Actually "The Butterfly's Ball and the Grasshopper's Feast," by the Liverpool poet William Roscoe.

ready for planting them as soon as they are opened. I shall write by this post to your Mama, so I conclude with my kisses to you all.

TH: JEFFERSON

Thomas Jefferson to His Granddaughter Ellen Wayles Randolph

Washington
Mar. 14. 08.

My dearest Ellen

Your letter of the 11th is received and is the best letter you have ever written me because it is the longest and fullest of that small news which I have most pleasure in receiving. With great news I am more than surfieted from other quarters, and in order that your letters may not be shortened by a bad pen of which you complain, I have got a pen for you which will be always good, never wearing or needing to be mended. Among my books which are gone to Monticello, is a copy of Madame de Sevigne's letters, which being the finest models of easy letter writing you must read. If Anne and yourself will take it by turns to write by every post, I shall always know of the health of the family; the first object of my concern. I am glad to learn you are at length likely to succeed with your Bantams. They are worthy of your attention. Our birds and flowers are well and send their love to yours. Mrs. S. H. Smith is also well; as I learn, for I have not seen her for a long time. She promises to visit us at Monticello this summer. I hope to be with you about the middle or latter part of April. The trumpet of war seems to have frightened the muses from our land or from some other cause they do not get admission into the newspapers of late. I hope this will find your Mama entirely recovered. Kiss her warmly for me, not forgetting the rest of the family. I salute you with love.

TH: JEFFERSON

Thomas Jefferson to Cornelia Jefferson Randolph

Washington, April 3, 1808

My Dear Cornelia,

I have owed you a letter two months, but have had nothing to write about, till last night I found in a newspaper the four lines which I now inclose to you: and as you are learning to write, they would be a good lesson to convince you of the importance of minding your stops in writing. I allow you a day to find out yourself how to read these lines, so far as to make them true. If you cannot do it in that time, you may call in assistance. At the same time, I will give you four other lines, which I learnt when I was but a little older than you, and I still remember.

> "I've seen the sea all in a blaze of fire
> I've seen a house high as the moon and higher
> I've seen the sun at twelve o'clock at night
> I've seen the man who saw this wondrous sight."

All this is true whatever you may think of it at first reading. I mentioned my letter of last week to Ellen, that I was under an attack of periodical headache. This is the 10th day. It has been very moderate, and yesterday did not last more than three hours. Tell your mamma that I fear I shall not get away as soon as I expected. Congress has spent the last five days without employing a single hour in the business necessary to be finished. Kiss her for me, and all the sisterhood. To Jefferson I give my hand, to your papa my affectionate salutations. You have always my love.

Th. Jefferson

P.S.—April 5. I have kept my letter open till today, and am able to say now, that my headache for the last two days has been scarcely sensible.

Thomas Jefferson to His Grandson Thomas Jefferson Randolph

Washington
Nov. 24th. 08

My dear Jefferson

I have just received the inclosed letter under cover from Mr. Bankhead which I presume is from Anne and will inform you she is well. Mr. Bankhead has consented to go and pursue his studies at Monticello, and live with us till his pursuits or circumstances may require a separate establishment. Your situation, thrown at such a distance from us and alone, cannot but give us all, great anxieties for you. As much has been secured for you, by your particular position and the acquaintance to which you have been recommended, as could be done towards shielding you from the dangers which surround you. But thrown on a wide world, among entire strangers without a friend or guardian to advise so young too and with so little experience of mankind, your dangers are great, and still your safety must rest on yourself.

A determination never to do what is wrong, prudence, and good humor, will go far towards securing to you the estimation of the world. When I recollect that at 14. years of age, the whole care and direction of my self was thrown on my self entirely, without a relation or friend qualified to advise or guide me, and recollect the various sorts of bad company with which I associated from time to time, I am astonished I did not turn off with some of them, and become as worthless to society as they were. I had the good fortune to become acquainted very early with some characters of very high standing, and to feel the incessant wish that I could even become what they were. Under temptations and difficulties, I could ask myself what would Dr. Small, Mr. Wythe, Peyton Randolph do in this situation? What course in it will ensure me their approbation? I am certain that this mode of deciding on my conduct tended more to it's correctness than any reasoning powers I possessed. Knowing the even and dignified line they pursued, I could never doubt for a moment which of two courses would be in character for them. Whereas seeking the same object through a process of moral reasoning, and with the jaundiced eye of youth, I should often have erred. From the circumstances of my position I was often thrown into the society of horseracers, cardplayers, Foxhunters, scientific and professional men, and of dignified men; and many a time have I asked myself, in the enthusiastic moment of the death of a fox, the victory of a favorite horse, the issue of a question eloquently argued at the bar or in the great Council of the nation, well, which of these kinds of reputation should I prefer? That of a horse jockey? A foxhunter? An Orator? Or the honest advocate of my country's rights? Be assured my dear Jefferson, that these little returns into ourselves, this self-cathechising habit, is not trifling, nor useless, but leads to the prudent selection and steady pursuits of what is right? I have mentioned good humor as one of the preservatives of our peace and tranquillity. It is among the most effectual, and it's effect is so well imitated and aided artificially by politeness, that this also becomes an acquisition of first rate value. In truth, politeness is artificial good humor, it covers the natural want of it, and ends by rendering habitual a substitute nearly equivalent to the real virtue. It is the practice of sacrificing to those whom we meet in society all the little conveniences and preferences which will gratify them, and deprive us of nothing worth a moment's consideration; it is the giving a pleasing and flattering turn to our expressions which will conciliate others, and make them pleased with us as well as themselves. How cheap a price for the good will of another! When this is in return for a rude thing said by another, it brings him to his senses, it mortifies and corrects him in the most salutary way, and places him at the feet of your good nature in the eyes of the company. But in stating prudential rules for our government in society I must not omit the important one of never entering into dispute or argument with another. I never yet saw an instance of one of two disputants convincing the other by argument. I have seen many of their getting warm, becoming rude, and shooting one another. Conviction is the effect of our own dispassionate reasoning, either in solitude, or weighing within ourselves dispassionately what we hear from others standing uncommitted in argument ourselves. It was one of the rules which above all others made Doctr. Franklin the most amiable of men in society, 'never to contradict any body.' If he was urged to announce an opinion, he did it rather by asking questions, as if for information, or by suggesting doubts. When I hear another express an opinion, which is not mine, I say to myself, He has a right to his opinion, as I to mine; why should I question it. His error does me no injury, and shall I become a Don Quixot to bring all men by force of argument, to one opinion? If a fact be misstated, it is probable he is gratified by a belief of it, and I have no right to deprive him of the gratification. If he wants information he will ask it, and then I will give it in measured terms; but if he still believes his own story, and shows a desire to dispute the fact with me, I hear him and say nothing. It is his affair, not mine, if he prefers error. There are two classes of disputants most frequently to be met with among us. The first is of young students just entered the threshold of science, with a first view of it's outlines, not yet filled up with the details and modifications which a further progress would bring to their kno[w]ledge. The other consists of the ill-tempered and rude men in society who have taken up a passion for politics. (Good humor and politeness never introduce into mixed society a question on which they foresee there will be a difference of opinion.) From both of these classes of disputants, my dear Jefferson, keep aloof, as you would from the infected subjects of yellow fever or pestilence. Consider yourself, when with them, as among the patients of Bedlam needing medical more than moral counsel. Be a listener only, keep within yourself, and endeavor to establish with yourself the habit of silence, especially in politics. In the fevered state of our country, no good can ever result from any attempt to set one of these fiery zealots to rights either in fact or principle. They are determined as to the facts they will believe, and the opinions on which they will act. Get by them, therefore as you would by an angry bull: it is not for a man of sense to dispute the road with such an animal. You will be more exposed than others to have these animals shaking their horns at you, because of the relation in which you stand with me and to hate me as a chief in the antagonist party your presence will be to them what the vomit-grass is to the sick dog a nostrum for producing an ejaculation. Look upon them exactly with that eye, and pity them as objects to whom you can administer only occasional ease. My character is not within their power. It is in the hands of my fellow citizens at large, and will be consigned to honor or infamy by the verdict of the republican mass of our country, according to what themselves will have seen, not what their enemies and mine shall have said. Never therefore consider these puppies in politics as requiring any notice from you, and always shew that you are not afraid to leave my character to the umpirage of public opinion. Look steadily to the pursuits which have carried you to Philadelphia, be very select in the society you attach yourself to; avoid taverns, drinkers, smoakers, and idlers and dissipated persons generally; for it is with such that broils and contentions arise, and you will find your path more easy and tranquil. The limits of my paper warn me that it is time for me to close with my affectionate Adieux.

Th: Jefferson

P.S. Present me affectionately to Mr. Ogilvie, and in doing the same to Mr. Peale tell him I am writing with his polygraph* and shall send him mine the first moment I have leisure enough to pack it.

Thomas Jefferson to Cornelia Jefferson Randolph

Washington, December 26, 1808

My Dear Corneila,

I congratulate you, my dear Cornelia on having acquired the valuable art of writing. How delightful to be enabled by it to converse with an absent friend, as if present! To this we are indebted for all our reading; because it must be written before we can read it. To this we are indebted for the Iliad, the Ænead, the Columbiad, Henriad, Dunciad, and now for the most glorious poem of all, the Terrapiniad, which I now enclose to you. This sublime poem consigns to everlasting fame the greatest achievement in war ever known to ancient or modern times; in the battle of David and Goliath, the disparity between the combatants was nothing in comparison to our case. I rejoice that you have learnt to write, for another reason; for as that is done with a goosequill, you now know the value of a goose and of course you will

---

*Polygraph: a machine using pens which made copies of a document.

assist Ellen in taking care of the half-dozen very fine grey geese which I shall send by Davy. But as I do this, I must refer to your mamma to decide whether they will be safest at Edgehill or at Monticello till I return home, and to give orders accordingly. I received letters a few days ago from Mr. Bankhead and Anne. They are well. I had expected a visit from Jefferson at Christmas, had there been a sufficient intermission in his lectures. But I suppose there was not, as he is not come. Remember me affectionately to your papa and mamma, and kiss Ellen and all the children for me.

Th. Jefferson

Thomas Jefferson to His Grandson Francis Wayles Eppes

Monticello
May 21. 16

I send you, my dear Francis, a Greek grammar, the best I know for the use of schools. It is the one now most generally used in the United States. I expect you will begin it soon after your arrival at the New London academy. You might, while at home, amuse yourself with learning the letters, and spelling and reading the Greek words, so that you may not be stopped by that when Mr. Mitchell puts you into the grammar. I think you will like him, and old Mr. and Mrs. Dehavens, from the character I have of them. I am sure Mr. Mitchell will do every thing for you he can and I have no fear that you will not do full justice to his institution. But, while you endeavor, by a good store of learning, to prepare yourself to become an useful and distinguished member of your country you must remember that this can never be, without uniting merit with your learning. Honesty, disinterestedness, and good nature are indispensible to procure the esteem and confidence of those with whom we live, and on whose esteem our happiness depends. Never suffer a thought to be harbored in your mind which you would not avow openly. When tempted to do any thing in secret, ask yourself if you would do it in public. If you would not be sure it is wrong: in little disputes with your companions, give way, rather than insist on trifles. For their love and the approbation of others will be worth more to you than the trifle in dispute. Above all things, and at all times, practice yourself in good humor. This, of all human qualities, is the most amiable and endearing to society. Whenever you feel a warmth of temper rising, check it at once, and suppress it, recollecting it will make you unhappy within yourself, and disliked by others. Nothing gives one person so great advantage over another, as to remain always cool and unruffled under all circumstances. Think of these things, practice them and you will be rewarded by the love and confidence of the world. I have some expectation of being at Poplar Forest the 3d. week of June, when I hope I shall see you going on cleverly, and already beloved by your tutor, curators, and companions, as you are by your's affectionately,

Th: Jefferson

Thomas Jefferson and Andrew Jackson to Thoms Jefferson Grotjan
Young Grotjan was one year old when Jefferson penned some appropriate sentiments to him at the request of his parents, who had named the boy for the former president. Nine years later, when President Jackson was passing through Philadelphia, Grotjan's father requested that Jackson add some sentiments of his own to the document.

Monticello
Jan. 10, [18]24

Th: Jefferson to Th: Jefferson Grotjan
Your affectionate mother requests that I would address to you, as a namesake[,] something which might have a favorable influence on the course of life you have to run. few words are necessary, with good dispositions on your part. Adore God, reverence and cherish your parents, love your neighbor as yourself; and your country more than life. be just, be true, murmur not at the ways of Providence, and the life into which you have entered will be the passage to one of eternal and ineffable bliss. and if to the dead it is permitted to care for the things of this world, every action of your life will be under my regard. farewell.

Philadelphia
June 9, 1833

Although requested by Mr. Grotjan, yet I can add nothing to the admirable advice given to his son by that virtuous patriot and enlightened statesman, Thomas Jefferson. The precious relic which he sent to the young child, contains the purest morality, and inculcates the noblest sentiments. I can only recommend a rigid adherence to them. They will carry him through life safely and respectably: and what is far better, they will carry him through death triumphantly; and we may humbly trust they will secure to all, who in principle and practice adopt them, that crown of immortality described in the Holy scriptures.

Andrew Jackson

JOHN QUINCY ADAMS (1825–1829)

Son of a president who demanded high standards from his children, John Quincy Adams was even more demanding and perhaps even more dour and humorless than his father. George Washington Adams (b. 1801), John Adams II (b. 1802), and Charles Francis Adams (b. 1807) were hectored as were few other children of their time, some of their epistolary education resulting from the long distances between father and sons. John Quincy was abroad for years as a diplomat, and when in office in Washington, he was often separated from his sons, who were at school or at home in Massachusetts.

From Russia, John Quincy, minister at St. Petersburg, not only wrote letters filled with the usual family news (mother, daughter, and youngest son were with him), but sent his two eldest sons, left at home with their grandparents, special lengthy treatises in the form of letters on reading the Bible. Although George, to whom they were addressed, was only ten when the lectures began, he was advised not only to read the Bible all the way through (his father claimed to do so once a year), but "in whatsoever you read, and most of all in reading the Bible . . . remember that it is for the purpose of making you wiser and more virtuous." Undoubtedly their mother, Louisa, agreed. For years, little of John Quincy's correspondence escaped her, as she copied, so she recalled, "all his private letters into his Letter Books to save his hand and Eyes, his Eyes being very weak, and his right hand . . . much on the tremble like his Fathers."

"Your letters are becoming a necessary of life to me," Adams once wrote to Charles Francis. He expected as many letters as he wrote, directing his sons' reading and recommending classical works that were for him, especially as harassed secretary of state or as president, "luxurious entertainment." Cicero, Pliny, Plato, and Pascal were less so for his sons. The epistolary style, he advised Charles Francis, had been useful for all kinds of literary works. One letter to him, John Quincy confessed, had been interrupted ten times through the evening by business, but he wrote on undeterred through the night, advising his son about men and morals. Napoleon, he cautioned, was, unlike Cromwell, only "a military and political gambler; playing every stake for himself; and doubling his stakes in utter defiance of the doctrine of chances, till it was impossible that he should not lose the game."

Despite the barrage of exhortations, not all went well with the Adams brood. George took part in a Harvard riot, and his father wrote an impassioned protest. Such preachments from a distance were useless in moving George to mend his ways. He gave up studying law, took to drink, fathered an illegitimate child by a servant girl, and died soon after by drowning, an apparent suicide. The tragedy occurred only two months after John Quincy had left the White House, embittered at his rejection and at the accession of Andrew Jackson—"a barbarian," Adams contended, "who could not write a sentence of grammar and hardly could spell his own name."

John Adams II appeared to have even less promise. His father complained about John's "grumbling" and "badly written" letters, once adding, with a misspelling, when John was fifteen, "Are you so much of a baby that you must be coaxed your Letters by sugar plumbs?" Then he prefaced his signature with "being always your affectionate, and whenever you deserve it, your indulgent father." After another student riot at Harvard, forty-three students were expelled, including young John. College students were younger then, but perhaps not better behaved.

Charles Francis was the only son to come to manhood without an "indolent" mind and likely to fulfill his father's hopes. He was a distinguished and effective minister to Great Britain during the troubled Civil War years and for a time had White House ambitions, but the second and sixth presidents were the only Adamses to occupy the office.

John Quincy Adams to His Son Charles Francis Adams

Washington
20 Nov. 1818

My Dear Son Charles
Your dear Mother not long since received a Letter from you, in which I read with great pleasure, that you get on at School pretty fast and that in three weeks you hope to begin College Studies. As it is just three weeks since you wrote that Letter, if your hopes have been fulfilled you will this very day begin upon Your College Studies, and Oh! how happy shall I be if you can hereafter write me with the sanctions of your teachers, you get on with them pretty fast. You know that when I was last at Boston and Jersey, I told you I should expect, you would be prepared, with the blessing of God to enter the University, in three years from the last Commencement. That you can be prepared in that time if you will take the pains I have not doubt.

There are many boys, with no better advantage than you enjoy who enter younger than you will then be and I know your capacity is equal to attaining in that time the necessary proficiency for it, if you will have this ambition to undertake it. I was disappointed in the wish I had to speak to Mr. Gould before I left Boston, and request him if he could consistently with the rules of his School, to put you into a Class where you would have a harder task with your lesson than you had where you were. You remember you yourself told me you could do more if you were in a higher Class. Now you may show Mr. Gould the letter and I am sure when he knows that you are willing to learn harder lessons than you [have,] he will if he can with propriety, indulge you with the opportunity of proving yourself equal to your promise.

We are yet in deep affliction my dear Charles, at the heavy loss we have met with in the decease of my ever honored Mother, who was to you and your Brothers as a Parent. I was just about your present age or perhaps a year younger, when her Mother, who like her was an Angel upon Earth, died. She had been kind, tender and affectionate to me, as your Grandmother has ever been to all my children; and now at this distance of more than 40 years I shall cherish her memory as that of one of the Dearest friends I have ever had in my life. It is pleasing though a melancholy remembrance that of virtuous friends who were the benefactors of our childhood, and though your long absence from this Country with your Parents has prevented you from partaking so long and so constantly as your brothers the tender solicitude and unwearied care of your departed Grandmother, yet it is not among the smallest of my consolations under this bereavement, that we were by a kind providence permitted to return from Europe, and to enjoy the happiness though but for a short time of society, and that you particularly have known her, and shared her kindness and affection to a degree, which will remain rooted in your heart, to the last hour of your life.

Give my love to your Brother John from whom your Mother yesterday received a very good Letter—and believe me your ever affectionate father—

JQA

John Quincy Adams to His Son John Adams II

Washington
17 November 1817

My dear John

I have received three Letters from you since I have been here, all grumbling Letters; and all very badly written. The first was of the 16th, the second of the 17th of September and the last of the 27th of October. This last I disapprove of the most; and request you to write me no more such Letters. You conclude it by saying that you hope I will forgive anything rash in my Son; but I shall do no such thing. If my Son will be rash he might take the consequences; and if my Son speaks or writes to me any thing disrespectful of his uncle, as you have done, he might not expect to be countenanced in it by me. You boast of your studying hard, and pray for whose benefit do you Study? Is it for mine or for your Uncle's? Are you so much of a baby that you must be coaxed to spell your Letters, by sugar plumbs? or are you such an independent Gentleman, that you can brook no control, and must have every thing you ask for? If so I desire you not to write for anything to me.

You say I know that in England the more I indulged you the more you studied and the better you behaved; but that is not my opinion. But this I know, that the more I indulged you the more you encroached upon my indulgence. The consequence is that now when you come to enter at Mr. Gould's you were so far behind what I expected, and even behind the boys of your own age at the same school. If you want more indulgence from me, you must deserve it; not only by close and constant attention to your studies, but by good conduct; by a chearful temper, and by respectful demeanour to your uncle, and to all my friends who have charge of you. Now you see I have answered your Letter as you required as soon as possible; and I hope you will enable me to answer your next Letter with more pleasure. Being always your affectionate, and whenever you deserve it, you[r] indulgent father

John Quincy Adams

John Quincy Adams to His Son George Washington Adams

Washington
December 1818

My Dear Son George

I received about a fortnight ago a few lines from you so ill written that it was with difficulty that I could read them and to my great surprize dated at

Quincy, when I had expected you were assiduously pursuing your studies at Cambridge after an interruption not less melancholy than indispensable. Your letter barely hinted at the temporary dissolution of your Class and by its brevity and obscurity left me to conjecture, that there had been nothing absolutely nothing in or warranted with the transaction which you would take satisfaction in communicating to me or that you imagined it would give me pleasure to know. I wrote you an answer, a Letter which at the request of your Mother, I omitted to send. She wrote you herself and from her Letter you will learn what sentiments were excited in my mind by the Event in which you had borne a share. Since your return to your duties at Cambridge I shall use with you no criminations or reproach. I am willing to flatter myself that you have had a Lesson of experience which will not be lost upon you and that through a process not very gratifying or very glorious to yourself you will come to the conclusion which I have so often and so earnestly endeavoured though as it appears without success to impress upon your mind by precept.

My dear George one of the earliest principles which that Angel, who is now gone to her own heaven inculcated upon my childhood, was [that] in all cases, throughout life, when a difficult choice was to be made between two different and opposite lines of conduct, to put the question to myself which was *right* and which was *wrong*—and if I could answer immediately that question, to inquire no further—to take the right side, and then to be moved from it by nothing upon Earth. After an experience of near half a century, there is no greater benefit and were I to die tomorrow there would be no better portion that I would bestow upon my children, than that same advise. Upon their attention to it, depend all my hopes of their future usefulness and prosperity.

When you returned to Cambridge after following the remains of one of your best and most affectionate friends, to the grave and found your Class engaged in a struggle against the College Government, in consequence of [a] transaction which had happened in your absence, and with which you had consequently nothing to do—did you before entering into the combination of your Class ask yourself that simple question? If you did, and deliberately took your stand in this roster of rebellion the Event has doubtless shewn you that you have yet something to do to attain maturity of judgement. But I think your capacity is not so small: that you had sense enough to know that you were doing wrong, but that you thought there was Spirit in setting the College Government at defiance, and good fellowship at least, in sharing the fortunes good or evil of your Class. You suffered yourself to be drawn into the contest, by the dint of importunity perhaps, and like Adam in the Paradise Lost preferred falling with your partners to standing erect in solitary virtue by yourself.

My purpose at present, I repeat, is not to reproach you with what is past and irredeemable. I regret that you lost the opportunity of exerting and exhibiting genuine Prudence and Firmness—because could I once see proof at a critical moment that you possessed those qualities, I should draw the conclusions that you possessed them for life, and should look forward with the most cheering hopes to the promise of your usefulness hereafter in the world. But next to consciousness of having done right under strong temptation to do wrong is the resolution of making past error turn to future profit. This is yet in your power and unpleasant as [is] the recollection of all that has happened in this affair may be, I advise you to dwell on it with the determination to improve your own heart and understanding in the Government of your future conduct. If you cannot learn to be wise from other's harm, at least do not let your own passions unheeded [fly] away. There will hereafter be no excuse for turning your eyes from the breakers, over that rock upon which you have once struck.

I never have known an instance of a combination among the Students at Cambridge avowedly for the purpose of resistance against the Government in which the Students were right. Without [my] saying that no such thing ever could happen, it may safely be affirmed that the presumption in every case of combination is violently against the students. Now I readily admit that among the Students at College and especially among those of the same Class there is a social connection which generates not only a common interest but also community of feelings laudable in itself, and pointing to duties which ought faithfully to be performed. These duties however have their bounds, and cannot extend to the sacrifice of other duties, prior to them in time and of higher and more solemn obligations. They are 1. the duty of observing the laws and regulations of the College—a duty not only proper in itself, but prescribed as a condition to which you assented at your admission, which you sanctioned by your deliberate promise and for which two of your friends, had become responsible for you by their bonds. 2. The duty of obedience to your Parents, who had enjoined upon you in the most correct manner, not only an entire observance of the College but of all just respect and deference for the Instructors and Officers of the Institution, and who had repeatedly warned you against entering into any combination for resistance whatever. 3. The duty of self respect—of regard to your own character—or preserving your own independence—of discharging your own obligations. All these were duties far superior to those of common interest and common feeling with your Classmates, and when brought into Collision with them upon so glaring a question as that of defiance to the authority of Government of the College, ought not to have allowed you one moment of hestitation, as to the course you should have pursued. But you chose to follow a multitude to do evil, and you have witnessed and shared the consequences.

I know not whether you will show more respect or pay more attention to these remarks than you have to my former admonitions concerning your conduct while at College. But I also have a duty to discharge to you as my Son. It is that of giving you faithful and affectionate advice especially for this Government of your conduct in difficult cases. Such are those in which personal inconvenience, obloquy, danger, the ill will, and resentment of others must follow to a certain extent the choice of either alternative to be pursued. Such was the case on the late occasion upon which you took the wrong side. Human life is full of such trying situations, and *character,* depends upon the manner in which they are met and passed through by individuals. The part you have taken in this instance proves that your character is not yet formed; but I do not dispair of its being formed hereafter. Raw troops who are siezed with a panic at the first sight of the Enemy and run away sometimes in the course of a campaign are found to stand without flinching at the charge of a bayonet. You have once suffered yourself to be led into folly. I will hope that the next time you will judge and act for yourself. If not—if from an inherent weakness of judgement or of nerves you are destined to be for life the sport of the passions and the victim of the vice of those with whom you may chance to be associated deeply as the wretchedness, which it will bring upon you, my sorrows will at least not be aggravated by the consciousness of having neglected to warn you of the fate to which such voluntary subserviency cannot fail to lead.

Your Mother and I had wished and intended that you should come and pass the Winter with us here, but as your company may be agreeable, and you may have an opportunity to make youself in some degree useful to your Grandfather, we are willing to forego the pleasure we had promised ourselves in seeing you here, until the next Season from the consideration that it will during the most tedious part of the year provide an additional comfort to him. We shall the more cheerfully submit to our privation, as we learn that Mrs. Clarke is coming to pass the Winter here, so that there will be only Cousin Louisa Smith left in the Family with your Grandfather, and we know that you can be in no possible situation better adapted to the improvement of the heart and the cultivation of your understanding than with him. We wish you therefore to make him the offer, and ask of him the favour of spending the vacation with him. And if you yourself should feel that you will thereby lose for the present the pleasure which you have anticipated in coming here, let it not escape your reflections that it will only be a postponement of what we hope you may enjoy with equal satisfaction and more profit the next Winter and that your privation now will not only be compensated by the excellent society of your Grandfather but by the meritorious consciousness of contributing to his comfort at this trying period of his distress.

I remain your ever affectionate Father
JQA

ANDREW JACKSON (1829–1837)

Andrew Jackson was the seventh president, after Madison, Monroe, and the second Adams. He had no children of his own. "Your heart, my love, will never be pierced by that cruel knife," General Jackson comforted his wife, Rachel, as they returned from one of the many funerals of neighbors' children. It was the only consolation he could give for their inability to have children. In compensation, they reared and educated at least eleven other children.

By 1809, when they legally adopted one of the twin sons born to Rachel's brother Sevren and his wife, Elizabeth, they were already the guardians of several wards, including Daniel, John, and Andrew Jackson Donelson, the son of Rachel's deceased brother Samuel. The adopted Andrew Jackson, Jr., came home to a Hermitage that also included among the Jackson wards the son of a neighbor, William Smith. In 1813, Jackson brought to the Hermitage and raised the three-year-old Lincoya, abandoned by the Creeks. Until his death from tuberculosis at fourteen, he was raised alongside Andrew, Jr. In 1815, Jackson added his last foster son to the family when he inherited Andrew Jackson Hutchings, the four-year-old child of his deceased former business partner (and Rachel's nephew), Maj. John Hutchings.

While doting on Andrew, Jr., and spoiling him shamelessly, Jackson did not neglect the other boys, showering on all of them love, attention, education, and money. When "Jack" Donelson attended Transylvania University, his uncle wrote to him at least once and frequently four times a week. After Andrew Hutchings, the baby of the brood, was expelled from his fourth school, Jackson financed his training as a plantation manager, at which he worked until he succumbed to tuberculosis. Refusing to permit Hutchings to take advantage of bankruptcy laws, which the scrupulous Jackson scorned, he spent much of his funds in bailing the dying man out of debts that the grave would have canceled.

Regretting his lack of a formal education, as his inconsistent spelling and punctuation reflect, Jackson insisted on the best schooling available for his wards, sending Edward Butler, Daniel Donelson, and Andrew Jackson Donelson to West Point, and Jack Donelson and later A. J. Donelson (on his leaving West Point) to Transylvania. At the time of Lincoya's death, Jackson was attempting to get him admitted to military school, and only after Hutchings's fourth expulsion did his guardian recognize that higher education was not the route for all young people.

As for the knife that never pierced the heart, Jackson suffered in his lifetime the death of three of his foster sons, Jack Donelson, Lincoya, and Hutchings, as well as the death of Hutchings's wife and baby. Jackson did not live to see four of the five young residents of the Hermitage die fighting for the Confederacy.

Andrew Jackson to Andrew Jackson Donelson

Nashville Febry 24 1817

Dear Andrew

Since writing to you yesterday, on reflection I have concluded, that your best plan will be to proceed on to West Point, taking Newyork on your west, where you will find Genl. Swift, to whom I have written by yesterdays mail and receive his instructions, as to the best plan for your government employment during the time that is to elapse before you can enter the m. academy. I have a great wish that you should be near West Point, where you can become acquainted with the rules & regulations of the academy, prepare yourself for your examination, & make such progress in the academical studies that will enable you to overtake, if not at once to join the senior class who has joined since last Sept^{br}. I enclose you a letter to my friend Mr Saml Cosswell which I request you to deliver yourself—it is open for your instruction—put a wafer [seal] in it before you deliver it. This will provide you the means of spending the summer, in the most beneficial mode for your future welfare & greatness.

My dear Andrew, you are now entered on the theatre of the world amonghst Stranger[s], where it behoves you to be guarded at all points. in your intercourse with the world you ought to be courteous to all, but make confidants of few, a young mind is too apt, to form opinions on speecious shows, and polite attention by others and to bestow confidence, before it has had proofs of it being well founded, when often, very often, they will be deceived, and when too late find to their Sorrow and regret that those specious shows of profered friendship, are merely to obtain confidence the better to deceive, you therefore must be careful on forming new acquaintances, how and where you repose confidence. I have full confidence in your Judgtment, when ripened with experience, I have full confidence in your morality & virtue. I well know, you will part with existance, before you will tarnish your honor, or depart from the paths of virtue and honesty. But you must recollect, how many snares will be laid for the inexperienced youth to draw him into disapation, vice and folly, against these snares I wish to guard you, This will be attempted first by obtaining your confidence, by specious display of, sacred reguard to virtue, honor and honesty, and deriding morallity and religion as empty hypocritical shows, endeavouring to draw you into little vices and dissapation, and step by step into those of a more destructive kind, from all which I wish you to be guarded. I do not mean by these observations, that you should, shut yourself up from the world, or depr[ive] yourself from proper relaxation, or innocent amusement but only, that you should alone intermix, with the better class of society, whose charactors are well established for their virtue, and upright conduct. Amonghst, the virtuous females, you ought to cultivate an acquaintance, and shun the intercourse of the others as you would the society of the viper or base charector—it is an intercourse with the latter discription, that engenders corruption, and contaminates the morals, and fits the young mind for any act of unguarded baseness, when on the other hand, the society of the virtuous female, enobles the mind, cultivates your manners, and prepares the mind for the achievement of every thing great, virtuous and honourable and shrinks from every thing base or ignoble. you will find Genl Swift in Newyork, when you reach there wait upon him and deliver the letter I gave you for him, take his instructions for your guide, I have requested his patronage for you under his admonitions, you are safe, from them I hope you will not depart.

I have barely to add, whilst I recommend oeconomy to you as a virtue, on the other hand shun parsomony never spend money uselessly, nor never withold it when necessary to spend it, I have notified Genl. Swift that you are authorised to draw on me for what sum of money may be necessary for your education and support.

All friends are well, & your aunt joins me in prayers for your health happiness & prosperity, & requests that you should write often—let me hear from you from Philadelphia before you leave that, from Newyork, & then from West Point as soon as you reach that place—& believe me to be affectionately your friend,

Andrew Jackson

P.S. Since writing the above I have mad[e] arrangements with Mr. James Jackson for any funds you may want & enclose you this note to Mr. Kirkman, which you will present—I have therefore not written to my friend Saml Cosswell as noted in this letter—but barely a letter of introduction to him.
A.J.

Andrew Jackson to Andrew Jackson Donelson

Hermitage Dec^{ber} 4th 1817

Dr Nephew

After an attendance of thirty odd days on our mutual friend, Major Hutchings, I closed his eyes on the 25th ult, in his sickness and Death he manifested that resolution and firmness that was always with him so conspicuous.

I reached Nashville on the 1st instant When I rec'd your letter of the 3rd ult. I am happy to find that order is restored in the academy—and that the envious & Malicious persecution of Capt. Pa[r]trid[g]e is about to recoil on the heads of his accusers, may he be honourably acquitted—and restored to the command of that place—present my good wishes to him.

I have duly noted the change the instruction has experienced under its new superintendant. I know your prudence—and seeing these things as you do, that you will do your duty faithfully and steer clear of either suspension or Dismissal. You have genius & application, these will soon give you promotion—and so soon as your studies are compleat should I live, I will endeavour to place you not only where you will be comfortable but where your talents will be most beneficial to your country and yourself. I have not rec'd a letter from Edward Butler, nor have you named him. I hope he has steered clear of eith[er] Dismissal or Suspension—but as he has not written, [n]or [have] you named him in your letter—I have some apprehension that all is not right—Pray inform me of him & of his health—present me affectionately to him and request him to write me.

Your friends are all well, your aunt and little Andrew desires to be affectionately presented. My faithful old servant Orange in my absence by accident has lost one of his legs, he is recovering.

I see from the changes you have pointed out, how much propriety there was in the caution I gave you when you first entered the academy—reflect on them, keep them locked in your bosom and read them on your pillow your reputation and Edwards are both as dear to me as my own—you cannot do a dishonourable act—but my Dear young friends, when you see how corrupt the world is grown, the fals[e]hood is resorted to by men high in office to tarnish the reputation of the honourable & innocent, how careful ought our step to be, to guard against the wickedness of mankind—with this remark I shall close this letter praying that the great god of the universe, will superintend you through your youthful walks & shield you from the scores of wicked men. I am your affectionate uncle
Andrew Jackson

Andrew Jackson to Andrew Jackson Donelson

State of Georgia Jackson County
Kolb[s] February 5th 1818

D[r] Nephew

I have no doubt but you have been surprised at my silence in not answering your letter of the 12th of Decbr. last, but when you look at the date of my letter and the place where written your astonishment will cease. I had a hope that I should have been permitted to have retired from the army without again having to forego, the fatigues & privations of a campaign in this inclement season in a wilderness—But on order from the president of the u states which reached me on the 12th of last month to repair to Ft. Scott, assume the immediate command of the troops there, concentrate the forces, call for any necessary artillery from the adjoining states, to give peace & security to our Southern frontier, under the order I am now on my way to Ft. Scott and expect to be joined in a few days after my arrival there with two Rgts of Volunteers from Tennessee—so soon as they arrive, I hope with the blessing of heaven, that I shall soon bring the Seminoles & their adherents to proper subjection & teach them that their safety solely depends on their remaining at peace with the u states—whether any other service than putting down the Seminoles may detour me on the southern frontier, time can only unfold.

My last letter ere this, has informed you that our friend Major John Hutchings is no more. He died on the 20th of Nov[br]—he left to my care his little son Andrew. I left the sweet little fellow with your aunt and our little son, all in good health.

I have had inclement weather & bad roads, and am at present inflicted with the Rheumatic pains—indeed my Dear Nephew I feel seriously the effects of the last campaign—my constitution is gone, and nothing but my fortitude left to bear me through this. I hope it will do for the present campaign, after which I will again apply for permission to retire from the army, for I never can bear the idea of asking for a furlough, or living on the publick bounty when unable to perform service.

I will be happy to hear from you, address me to Ft. Hawkins. It will reach me. Present me to Edward Butler—say to him I have not time to write him, I write this with bad light and on my knees—I wish to remind you both of the great anxiety I have for your wellfare & Preferment, application alone can secure it to you. I am, Dr Andrew with sincere regard your affectionate uncle

Andrew Jackson

Andrew Jackson to Andrew Jackson Hutchings

Jackson's ward was a student at the University of Virginia. The president clearly realized that Hutchings was not doing well and feared the worst.

Washington
November 15, 1831

My D'r Hutchings,

I have not received a line from you for the last three weeks, how this has happened I am at a loss to account. One inch of a candle more than is burnt in your usual studies, would remedy the neglect I complain of, if applied in writing to me. Am I mistaken? if I am not, then, you did promise to write me once every week. the pleasure I assured you, of hearing from you weekly, and judging your improvement from your composition, I had a hope would have been a sufficient inducement to your fulfilment of this promise. Hoping that you have a good excuse for this neglect, I shall waive further comment at present, looking to a faithful fulfilment on your part for the future.

I am perfectly recovered from the attack of fever, and my strength quite restored, I am more free from affliction than I have been for years, for which I am thankful to the great giver of all good, to whom we are daily indebted for his protection and preservation.

Mr Trist has informed me that you suggested to him a desire you had to visit me in the christmas holidays. I will be happy to see you then, and if it should be necessary for me to request this indulgence from the professors, I will address them a note upon this subject; inform me on this point.

My son is to be married on the 24th instant to Miss Sarah York of Philadelphia, said to be, by my friends who have wrote me on the subject, accomplished, amiable, beautiful. these qualities must insure his happiness, or the fault must be his, and in his welfare and happiness mine measurably consists. therfore my full approbation is given. I cannot yet say when he will return, but I suppose in a few days after their marriage, when I would be happy you could be here, and become acquainted with your adopted cousin.

I am D'r Andrew with sincere regard your affectionate
Andrew Jackson

Andrew Jackson to Andrew Jackson Hutchings
On February 11, 1832, Jackson received word at the White House, "with heartfelt mortification," that his ward was on the verge of expulsion for excessive absences from class. Hutchings decided to withdraw on his own accord. Though he was disappointed and embarrassed, Jackson wrote to his friend Gen. John Coffee:

> On receipt of this information, fearing he might be without funds, I wrote him to advise me of his wants, and I would supply them for his return to Tennessee. he wrote me he had wrote you for funds, and I am happy to learn you have forwarded them. I requested him to come by this place, on his way to Tennessee. by a letter wrote to him to my son and recd to[-]day he declines coming here, and I suppose will soon be with you, as he writes me, he intends going to his place and residing there. I am happy to learn from the professors, that his moral conduct is without blemish, that he had failed to attend three recitals, and was, I suppose, severely lectured upon this subject, and threatened with expulsion, and he with three others, I understood, withdrew. Hutchings says, the professor of one branch of his studies was sick, and failed to attend, and reported them absent, when he was not there to hear them. Be this as it may, I am happy to inform you that he stands remarkably high in the estimation of all his fellow students, and the citizens of Charlottesville. he has improved very much, both in his size and education, and I have no doubt now, but he will apply himself to his farm, and if he does, and gets a few good books, a well selected little library, he will be a useful citizen; but he cannot bear the subordination of a university. he has talents but as yet, lacks application.

Washington, D.C.
February 11, 1832

My dear Hutchings,

How humiliating to my feelings this intelligence! How useless has [been] my various admonitions, and your promises to me when last here, that your application should be redoubled, and your obedience to all the rules of the university strictly observed, if I would permit you to visit Philadelphia. I have been unwearied in my attention to have you given a first rate education. My solicitude that you should come well into life, could not have been exceeded by your D'r father who bequeathed you to me. But enough. My present solicitude is to know where you are. Your determination being taken to withdraw from the university without my knowledge and consent, and your want of funds to take you home, has doubled that solicitude. There is one, and only one consolation left me, and that is, that you stand accused of no moral delinquency. Your moral character being still maintained I can forgive and take you to my bosom again. On the receipt of this you will apprise me of your pecuniary situation, the amount that will close all your accounts, and take you to Tennessee, where you will await my further instructions after you receive the funds to take you there.

I am D'r Andrew with sincere regard your affectionate
Andrew Jackson

Andrew Jackson to Andrew Jackson Hutchings

At eighteen, Hutchings found himself back on the family farm, near Jackson's own Tennessee plantation, the Hermitage. By the next year, he had taken hold, and Jackson had forgotten his earlier humiliation in the desire to convey a fund of parental counsel.

Washington
April 18, 1833

Dear Hutchings,

I am at last gratified in receiving a letter from you. yours of the 5th instant has just been received, and I sincerely thank you for the information given of the family and of the state of the Hermitage. I sincerely regret the loss of the two Sampsons, as I do the rest, but where it does not arise from neglect, or inhumanity, but from the will of our creator, "who giveth, and has the right to take away", I submit to it, with an humble resignation. I was fearful from a letter I had received from a connection, that there might be neglect and particularly in the death of Titus, and Anake, Ben's daughter. When you see Mr. Holtzclaw say to him I have recd your letter, and am pleased with the description you give me of the contentment of the negroes and the situation of the farm, and stock, and hope it will long continue.

I am happy to find you have taken the management of your estate into your own hands. I have only once more to remark to you, that you will find many who will profess much friendship, court you with kindness to obtain your confidence if they can, and then obtain your money, and swindle you out of it, if possible. therefore, act as tho you had confidence in all, never reposing it in any until you have good reason to believe, it will be well placed. deal with all as tho' they were dishonest and you never can be deceived, because the honest man deceived no one, and you will then be all-ways guarded against the dishonest.

Major Lewis was advised by me that you would want your money this spring. He said to me in reply, that if you did, he would arrange his matters to pay you in Nashville: he is now there. Doctor Hogg will certainly pay you, or secure the debt by giving you a new bond with security. I wish to close all your business in such a manner as will put you in receipt of all the money due the estate. Doctor Hogg is in honor bound to secure this debt, and pay it punctually. I had a lien on his property, but trusting to his honor as I still do, I let it go for his benefit and I wish you, as soon as possible, to have it secured: he can pay it, if he will. he can, I should suppose, get it from the Bank. he is in good practice and must have a great deal of money owing to him and if you think it doubtful, I would advise you to take good notes from him at such discount as will indemnify you in the trouble and expence of collecting it. I inclose a note to the Doctor open for you to read, seal and deliver to him.

. . . See all my colts and tell me how they look. how does my Citizen stud colt look? is he large and likely, what is the promise of his colt by the Oscar filly, and compare it with the Boliver out of Diana, the virginian, and let me know really how Mr. Holtzclaw is getting on, and how the negroes are, and if contented. how much cotton is planted, and how much corn, and how the whole crop, wheat, grass, oats and rye looks, with a glance at the sheep, horned cattle and hoggs. and how all our friends are, and good neighbors, etc.

If you have leisure please tell me is Mr. Albert Ward serious in proposing his place for sale and if he is, at what price. I would be happy to hear of you often and particularly how your farm, negroes, crop and stock are progressing, whether your overseer is doing well and the amount of your last years crop of cotton. my crop has not paid half its expence and left me the farm $380 in debt. So much for my absence. Tell me what Thomas J. Donelson is doing and the Doctor. Samuel graduated with credit at Philadelphia and obtained his diploma. I am afraid Thomas will be disappointed in the expected fortune, and perhaps Emma thought she was getting a fortune. She has in the man, I am sure, if not in guinies.

One word to you as to matrimony—seek a wife, one who will aid you in your exertions in making a competency and will take care of it when made, for you will find it easier to spend two thousand dollars, than to make five hundred. Look at the economy of the mother and if your find it in her you will find it in the daughter. recollect the industry of your dear aunt, and with what economy she watched over what I made, and how we waded thro the vast expence of the mass of company we had. nothing but her care and industry, with good economy could have saved me from ruin. if she had been extravagant the property would have vanished and poverty and want would have been our doom. Think of this before you attempt to select a wife. when you can find such, and I think you can, then would I say to you that you cannot too soon settle yourself.

For economy and prudence I would bring to your view Genl Coffee and Polly. take Coffee for your guide, receive his admonitions and pursue them, and you will be sure to do well. live within your means, never be in debt, and by husbanding your money you can always lay it out well, but when you get in debt you become a slave, therefore, I say to you never involve yourself in debt, and become no mans surety. If your friend is in distress aid him if you have the means to spare. if he fails to be able to return it, it is only so much lost, your property is not sold by the sheriff to raise it, as is the case when you become security and have to pay the debt, that you have made no provisions to meet. think of all these things. practice them as you enter life and they will end your days in pleanty and in peace. I say live always within your means—settle all your debts on the first of every year and you will know your means, and can keep within it. . . .

Your affectionate

Andrew Jackson

Andrew Jackson and Martin Van Buren to Miss Rachel Jackson

Both President Jackson and Vice President Van Buren wrote notes to Jackson's granddaughter for inclusion in an album presented to her in December 1835 by Martin Van Buren.

The following short admonition is written for the meditation of my Dear Little Rachel Jackson by her affectionate Grandpa, with a hope that as her little mind matures by age, she will meditate upon it, and make it a guide for her riper years. In early life, search for truth and learn wisdom from the precepts as laid down in the Holy Scriptures—This, my dear child will make smoothe the path of life and at last, lead you to a happy immortality.

March 30th 1836.
Andrew Jackson

I am very thankful to my friend Mrs. Jackson for the opportunity she has afforded me to add my prayers for the happiness of her dear little daughter to those of her venerable GrandPa.

M. Van Buren
Washington April 1836

Andrew Jackson to Alice Egerton

The former president was ailing and three years from his death when he responded to a girl's request for a lock of his hair. With the letter survives a copious lock of white hair, sewn onto a piece of silk.

Hermitage
October 25, 1842

Miss Alice Egerton
My Dear Miss,
Your very interesting and pious letter of the 10th instant is before me; and for that pious benediction which it conveys for my temporal, & spiritual happiness, receive my thanks, and my sincere reciprocation of them.

You request a lock of my hair, —with pleasure I comply with that request, and herein inclose it.

I rejoice to find by your letter that you have adopted that true wisdom and valuable precept, "in youth is the time to serve the Lord," continue to walk in this path thro' life, and it will lead you to a glorious immortality, where I trust, resting on the atonement of our blessed Saviour, I shall meet you in the realms of bliss.

I am greatly debilitated, write with great difficulty, and can only add my prayer for your long & useful life & a happy immortality.

Andrew Jackson

MARTIN VAN BUREN (1837–1841)

Martin Van Buren, Jackson's vice president, was the first of three descendants of early Dutch settlers of New York to become president. (The others were the two Roosevelts.) The only letters from him to children that survive are slightly more than a half dozen to his own children written before he attained the White House. At the time of Van Buren's election in 1836, only his youngest of four sons, Smith Thompson, remained a minor. He had been two years old when his mother, Hannah Van Buren, died in 1819.

Rearing his motherless sons while conducting a political career was not easy for Van Buren. Coping with his unruly second son, John, was especially difficult. All but one of Van Buren's extant letters to children are to John, most of them deploring his lack of manners, carelessness with money, and early drinking habits. Still, "Prince John," as he was mockingly called, survived his early indiscretions. Only ten years after Van Buren's letters of fatherly concern, John was elected to the House of Representatives—in the same election in which Van Buren as incumbent president was defeated for a second term. The tone of the letters to John differs considerably from that of the letter to young Smith. In the letters to John appear a father dismayed by his son's failures, including academic and disciplinary trouble at school and reckless spending. Yet only seven years later, the formerly anxious father is shown seeking financial advice from his son, who had turned his life around. In the letter to Smith, perhaps the longest that Van Buren wrote to any of his children, the tone is relaxed, even gossipy and affectionate.

Martin Van Buren to John Van Buren

Washington
January 19 1826

My dear Son

I am as you supposed somewhat surprised to hear that you went direct to Greenbush. I wrote you advising you to go to Kinderhook & to visit Albany from thence. I know the kindness which induces Mr & Mrs Duer to wish to have you at their house, & approve your taste for [being] pleased with the good society you meet there, but I fear your Kinderhook friends will think themselves neglected as I think they may well. You know the pain it give[s] me [to] express dissatisfaction with your conduct, but I would do injustice to both, were I not to say that the account you give me of your expenditures is far from satisfactory.

You say you have spent $150 in six weeks, & instead of giving me an account of it, or even speaking of its absolute necessity, you tell me of the expenditures of other boys, & the declarations of Js. Backness as to how much he had spent. You have nothing to do with the expenses of other Boys. When I proposed to make you the depository of your funds, I did so, (you know) agt the opinion & advice of others. My wish was to excite your ambition to shew that you were free from the weakness of other boys in this respect, & more deserving of confidence than they too often are. I endeavored to impress you sensibly on this point, and assured you solemly, that the moment I had reason to apprehend that my confidence was not safely placed, I would withdraw it. I will not judge you definitively until I hear from you, but if the account you give me of your disbursements is not such as it should be, I shall assuredly, promptly, & peremptorily change my course, & leave it to Mr. Croswell to advance you from time to time what money you may want—Let me therefore hear from you directly upon this subject.

I sincerely hope you will be able to explain to me this matter fully as I shall be uneasy until you do so—

The money is the least, by far the least, of my concern—

Make my most affectionate regards to Mr & Mrs Duer & all the children—

Your affectionate father
M V Buren

Martin Van Buren to S. T. Van Buren

Washington
January 5 1835

My dear Son

I owe you an apology for not having sooner answered your letter asking information in regard to which my interest is only next to yours. Instead of laying down particular rules for your course of reading as desired, either from my own course or the suggestions of after experience I will make an observation or two, which, will if properly improved, be more servicable to you. First then I am sensible that I lost much valuable time in deliberating upon and discussing the superior advantages of one course over an other, & that the benefits of my studies were greatly lessened by the changes to which my reading was subjected from the speculation & schemes which I dwelt upon in regard to the best way of getting along in the matter. 1st That if instead of troubling myself with cogitations upon that point I had taken up the first of the usual books that I met with, such as Blackstone, Coke etc & read it honestly & continuously, I would have succeeded much better. 2nd That the only way to acquire a fondness for law is to read constantly—a month's study is rendered comparatively unprofitable by a month's abstinence. You return to it with reluctance, whilst if you keep constantly at it your fondness for it increases, & your capacity to comprehend & improve what you read as constantly expands. 3d That it is of great advantage to apply your reading, as often as possible, (though by no means exclusively), to some particular case arising in the office, & in which you naturally, from you knowledge of the parties, etc. take an interest. When therefore you find a case coming in the office, ascertain what questions of law arise in it & give to that question a thorough examination,—Test [them as well] by general principles as adjudged cases—make a brief of your reflections & authorities, and you will soon come to take such an interest in the case as will induce you to attend the argument & to keep your eye upon the decisions. Impressions thus made will be lasting—the great object as well as the great difficulty in studies like that of the law. The Elementary treatises have so greatly multiplied since I left the profession that my judgment in regard to the course of your general reading would be of less value than those of others within your rank—Mr. Butler for instance. I am however confident that a course something like this could not fail to be eminently useful. 1st Take for instance Blackstone's Commentaries—read a chapter—make a full note of the principles of law it contains. 2nd Read what the Revised laws contain upon those points and note them also. 3ly. Read Kent's commentaries and note the new lights which they throw upon the particular principles before you. 4th Ascertain how far the rule laid down by Blackstone has been confirmed, modified or changed by the decisions of our Courts, & wind up in the matter by a brief statement of the results, that is, how the law upon these points now stands. This summary you will be likely to remember—The search will stimulate you, & when you have gotten through one chapter in this way you will approach the next with a gratifying conviction that you have derived advantage from what is past—as well in establishing in your mind some principles is in your increased capacity to understand with greater facility what is to come. But after all the great secret is to acquire a fondness for reading and investigations, & that can only be acquired by keeping at it. You cannot reason yourself or resolve yourself into it. On the contrary if you do but keep at it you cannot help growing fond of it. This I know by actual experience & I know also that I sustained incalculable injury by putting off from time to time the beginning of the business to be better advised as to the mode of prosecuting it, for more time and better opportunities. etc. etc. This I have done—this John has done & this you will do unless you make a great exertion to avoid it.

I have scratched this off waiting for my carriage at the Capitol & as that has arrived I must close. I have given your message to the Genl who reciprocates your compliments very sincerely. Matters are all going on here as well as could be expected or desired. Your *old* flame is not here but expected. The Major is the same two & six pence & we have a large & really elegant dinner every Saturday. Now as I have answered your questions let me put you one in regard to my old flame—Did you express to Miss Brinckerhoff my regrets at not seeing her before I left Albany! If not do so & say that she won the hearts of Genl. & Mrs. Gratiot who have been here singing her praises very lustily. As you cannot know what may happen you would not be exercising your usual prudence to be guilty of neglect in this quarter. The old chief is well but getting rather belligerent ag[ains]t Louis Philippe. Remember me very kindly to the Patroon* and his ladies & to all my particular friends at Albany. Write me often and long for your letters are very interesting to me & it costs you no effort to write them. Martini often expresses a desire to see you & it would be very gratifiying to him to get a letter from you. Tennessee is getting along bravely. Mrs. Camberleng is admitted on all points to be a marvelously proper lady. etc. etc.

I have had an application to buy a part of the whole of my Oswego property. Ask John whether it would be safe for me to take $80,000 or $75,000 for an undivided half. We wait with impatience for the Govs message. Tell Jane [I] know that if it is not full & strong upon the abolition question I will hold her responsible for the omission. We are all in love with *Cassum* & so is everybody else as far as I can hear. Love to John—and believe me to be very truly yours

       M. Van Buren
       Washington Jany 5 1835

[Addendum on envelope:]
"The longest & best letter that I ever recd from this quarter. If any one desires to know the date it will be found within."

---

*The Patroon is the eldest Van Rensselaer, Stephen, the recognized head of the descendants of the Dutch community along the Hudson.

JOHN TYLER (1841–1845)

John Tyler became the first "accidental president," when the elderly hero of the Battle of Tippecanoe, Gen. William Henry Harrison, died after a month in office. Before Tyler had run with Harrison, he had been governor of Virginia, then a senator. Although professedly a Jacksonian, Tyler was actually a conservative, aristocratic lawyer-planter. His pre-presidential letters to his first family (he was widowered while in the White House and remarried) suggest that he was widely read, sophisticated in outlook, and affectionate to his children, who were distant from Washington in Tidewater Virginia. Of his eight children by Letitia, the sixth, Anne, died in 1825 when three months old, and Tyler composed a poetic lament for her, "child of my love," calling her "born for a day" but "enveloped in night." The elder children were closest to him emotionally, as they were already able to write when the enforced separation that political life in Washington required in days of poor travel conditions kept them apart.

At first from Mrs. McDaniels's boardinghouse in Washington and then from his Senate desk, the president-to-be guided his children by letter, oversaw his plantation, and responded to their adolescent problems. He encouraged them to participate in the social life of nearby Williamsburg and Richmond, and he sent them money to fund their attendance at parties and balls, telling his elder sons that "polish and shape to manners . . . constitute one-half the concern in our journey through life. I have known persons possessing only ordinary capacities getting on better than others who were in intellect greatly superior, simply for force of manners."

The children were tutored and schooled to the limit possible for the area and time, and Tyler encouraged additional study, once threatening to send Mary Tyler fifty volumes of Voltaire—in French. He also molded their political views to reflect his own states' rights faith, and after his presidency they were loyal both to Virginia and—during the Civil War—to the Confederacy. His personal integrity was so profound that he would not use his franking privilege for private mail within the family—a concern later associated with the presidency of Harry Truman. Yet he exploited his influence in a manner he judged politically acceptable to secure patronage jobs for members of his family.

Tyler's new first lady was the nation's youngest. Julia Gardiner, of a prominent New York family, was twenty-four and beautiful. She and the new brood that the president, now past sixty, began outlived Tyler by many decades.

John Tyler to Mary Tyler
His daughter was twelve when then Senator John Tyler wrote to her about the nation's capitol, which she had not yet seen. The exhortations about handwriting and manners sound Jeffersonian.

Washington
Dec. 26, 1827

My Dear Mary:
Your letter of last week reached me too late in the week to enable me to reply to it earlier than this. I need not say to you that it afforded me pleasure. You should write to me frequently—every week would not, in fact, be too often, since it would tend to improve your hand and style. A young lady should take particular pains to write well and neatly, since a female cannot be excused for slovenliness in any respect. You should never feel cramped in writing. Write as you would converse, and give your mind free play. Be not afraid to reflect, and write down your reflections as they occur. If you have no neighborhood incidents to relate, give an account of your studies, and dwell on the prominent occurrences of history, expressing your own notions of the characters and actions which figure in history. Thus shall I be enabled to judge your progress, and bear witness to the expansion of your mind. The history of Greece is the book you should now read; and when you open it, do so with the resolution to understand it.

You desire me to give you an account of the capitol. This I must postpone until I see you. The building is now nearly finished, and is very splendid. It is so large that I have nearly lost myself in it two or three times. What principally attracts attention is the large central dome, which is about two hundred feet in circumference, and is ornamented with works of the brush and chisel. Over each door is seen some emblematical representation of incidents connected with our early history. One of them exhibits Captain Smith with his head on a rock; Powhatan with a club over him, and Pocahontas interposing to save his life. This, I think, is the best. In another William Penn is exhibited with three Indians, who have made the treaty ceding to him Pennsylvania. The others I do not now recollect. There are four paintings by Trumbull,—a book explanatory of which I will bring on with me when I come.

Why did not some of you write to me by the last mail? Are you all so much taken up with your Christmas frolics as to have forgotten me? This I cannot believe, and yet I do think that your mother might have stolen one hour to devote to me. I do not suffer anything to prevent my writing every week. Tell her that I have attempted in every way to account for her neglect. Company would not prevent me from writing to her. She may have gone to Mrs. Savage's wedding, and yet how easy was it for her to have written, and sent the letter to Frazier's. However, if Providence permits, I shall be at home on Sunday week, and will then listen to her excuses. I wish to leave this so as to reach Richmond on Saturday evening, and to take the steamboat on Sunday morning. Tell the overseer to send a canoe or boat around to River-Edge on Sunday by the time that the boat reaches there (Sunday the 6th January). I went yesterday (Xmas day) to the Catholic church, where they performed high-mass. The preacher said that Christmas took its name from *Christ* and *mass*, and hence inferred that mass should always be observed on that day. The ceremonies were very long, but I could not understand them,—their prayers are sung out in Latin. The sermon was a good one. On the same day I dined with Mr. Cary Selden, a brother of Jas. Selden's. Several gentlemen were there, and after dinner Miss . . . and her brother danced a waltz,—a dance which you have never seen, and which I do not desire to see you dance. It is rather vulgar, I think.

Tell your mother that I returned Mr. Randolph's visit, and was received in a style somewhat stately, but entirely respectful; since when I have received another card from him. He conversed in a low whisper, and said that he labored under pulmonary consumption. All here is quiet, and we are getting on smoothly.

I shall not write again until I reach home, unless something occurs to postpone my trip, but shall expect to receive letters by the next mail.

With my love to all, I am, dear daughter,

Your affectionate father,
John Tyler

John Tyler to Mary Tyler

Away in Washington alone, Tyler often wrote his children, addressing the letter to one of the eldest, then adding postscript admonitions for some of the younger children.

Washington
April 30, 1828

Dear Mary:
Your letter reached me on Sunday. Although your style is still cramped, yet you are certainly improving very much. Why did you not give the number of votes which your Uncle William and Mr. Graves received? I should also have been gratified at learning the state of the poll for a convention. I suppose you know what that means; but lest you should not, I must tell you that the votes of the people are now taken in order to ascertain whether there be a majority in favor of changing the Constitution of the State government—I mean a majority of all the freeholders of the State. If there is, then delegates will be elected to meet at some future day, whose business it will be to revise, alter or amend the present Constitution of the State. Various amendments are spoken of—one is to do away with the Executive Council, and give the governor more power; another is to elect delegates to the Assembly according to some general rule of numbers; this would seem to be just, since Charles City, with but one hundred and eighty votes, has as much weight in the General Assembly as the county of Shenandoah with its one thousand two hundred votes; that is to say, Charles City sends two delegates and Shenandoah but two. This seems to be unjust. Other changes are to be proposed.

Now think on this until you understand it, and let it not be said that a great movement is going on in the country which you do not understand. Tell Mr. Robert the same thing. In short, my dear daughter, you should always try to understand everything you hear talked of, for it is only in that way that you will ever acquire much knowledge.

As to the reason which led Mr. Adams to give "Ebony and Topaz" for a toast, no one can say, unless indeed it was to show his learning. The story which you have read is an excellent moral tale, and one you should always recollect. There are, according to it, two genii who always attend upon us— the one good, the other evil. The first Voltaire calls Topaz; the last Ebony. The first is evermore resisting the last. The last is constantly tempting us from the path of virtue and morality, and in order to do so, spreads before us the most captivating illusions. The first whispers in our ears that vice can never give any real lasting pleasure, but is followed by certain destruction. Ebony speaks the language of the passions, Topaz that of reason. Listen to Ebony, and you will be ruined; to Topaz, and you will not fail to be happy and respected. The Scriptures represent these genii under the names of *Satan* and *eternal goodness*. They both mean the same thing, and teach us to restrain our tempers and dispositions, always asking ourselves before we commit any action, is it right, is it proper, is it virtuous, is it honorable? This I fondly hope my children will do through life, and Ebony, or the spirit of darkness, will exercise no power over them.

Mr. Robert: You say you could find nothing to write to me about. Could you not have told me how the corn had come up, how it looked, how the wheat looked, how many lambs there were, how many times Mr. Vaiden had whipped you, and whether you were able to keep up with your cousin John in Latin?

Learn to write exactly as you would talk, since the writing a letter is nothing more than conversing with one who is too far off to hear you. None of you said a word about John or Letty, nor of the baby. You might have let me know whether she was handsome or not. But practice makes perfect, and so you must write to me often, and don't think so much of play. Give my love to John, Letitia and Elizabeth, and when you write next, Mary, make them sit down and send me messages.

Your father,
John Tyler

John Tyler to Mary Tyler

Washington
April 28, 1830

My Dear Daughter:

Your letter of the 23d instant is now before me, and, although it is somewhat short, yet it certainly deserves an answer. Before I proceed to express to you the pleasure it gave me, I must point out to you two errors into which you have fallen. The river *Rhone* is spelt with an *h*, but not so with James *Roane*. You turned him into a river by your mode of spelling his name. And you say that "this is a great letter to be sent *a* 150 miles." Thus you conclude your letter. Now the *a* is out of place, and cannot be the antecedent to "miles." You would say *a mile,* but not *a miles.* I mention this to make you more attentive to your grammar. The mistake occurring with me makes no odds, but if you had been writing to any one else it would be terrible.

To write with facility requires practice. You should, therefore, write every week whilst I am here. You can never be at a loss for a subject if you will but get rid of the idea that you are to *look out for news*. Incidents which arise in the neighborhood do very well to communicate; but then you own reflections on what you read and on what you converse about would always afford you matter enough for a letter to me.

The character of Sir Roger de Coverley is one of the best ever drawn of a real country gentleman. Might you not have touched off the finest traits of his character? So in regard to anything that you read. Learn, my dear daughter, to criticize the style, manner, and subject of the author, and you will read to great advantage. In reading the history of England, notice particularly the advance made to liberty, both of action and of conscience. The king was once supreme, and his will was law. The people were considered his vassals, and their liberties were next to nothing until King John was made to sign *Magna Carta (the great charter.)* The Bill of Rights was afterwards obtained. From these two sources flow the liberty of England as enjoyed at the present day; and from them, too, came our freedom, for we have incorporated their principles with our laws. The representation of the people in parliament furnished our forefathers with their notions of free government. The king, you know, can get no money but through parliament. Thus the people are not liable to unjust taxes. The trial by jury is justly considered the great bulwark of English and American liberty. In Turkey the subject holds his property and his life at the mere pleasure of the sultan. But not so in England or here. My neighbors have to decide whether I have violated the laws or not, and in their hands I feel myself safe.

These remarks will enable you to understand the history better. Think of what you read, and you will not forget. You should think as much as you read. Do not neglect your philosophy and chemistry. Look over them, and you can say them to yourself. The *"Tatler"* is as good a book as you can now read. It is, however, not equal to the *"Spectator."* Johnson's "Lives of the Poets" are very instructive and amusing. You will find them among *"The British Classics."* In truth, knowledge is all around you, inviting you to taste of her sweets. Pope, Gray, Goldsmith, Johnson, Addison, Milton, and others are ready to pour upon your mind the rich treasures of knowledge. Profit by them, my daughter, and it will be a source of comfort to you through life.

I am reading Moore's "Life of Lord Byron." He was, in very truth, the soul of poetry; but he was a singular man. I hope you have received your music. Chapman wrote me that it was recovered with the saddle-bags. Do not fail to write very often.

Your affectionate father,
John Tyler

Let Robert and John read this.

John Tyler to Robert Tyler

             Washington
             Feb. 2, 1832

My Son:

 Your last letter gives me further evidence of your application to your studies, and therefore affords me much pleasure. To witness your advance in knowledge, and that of your sisters and brothers, will constitute the charm of my future life, and so far I have much reason to be satisfied. Your admiration of the style of Hume is every way just, for undoubtedly few writers have ever equalled him; but what then?—are all others to be thrown aside because they cannot rival him in beauty and richness? This will not do, for then your reading would become too circumscribed. Smollett is very inferior in both these respects, but he nevertheless gives you a true narrative of facts; and you are now in pursuit of *facts*. You want a knowledge of the history of England, and you can only obtain that knowledge by reading the books containing it. Do not halt, therefore, because the writer may be somewhat dull or prolix, but encounter him with resolution, resolving to get from him, for the labor he imposes, all he can give you. I would have you form your own style upon the chaste and pure model of Swift, Addison and Hume; but these are *rarae aves in terra,*—all admire, while few attain their excellence.

 The newspapers are full of the rejection by the Senate of Mr. Van Buren as minister to England. Mr. Tazewell and myself voted for him, and now the papers that have all along abused us come out in our praise. Mr. Ritchie cannot, however, praise us equally. He extols Mr. Tazewell most without knowing anything of the part which I have borne. The truth is, that from the first of the session I have exerted myself to procure his confirmation. While I admitted that much of suspicion attached to him on account of recent occurrences, yet I did not think it wise or proper to rest on mere suspicion in rejecting him. He was qualified for the place, and I therefore voted for him.

 The *Globe,* a paper published here, and established by Van Buren, after having greatly abused us heretofore, comes out now and extols, and talks of the *moral influence of the Virginia senators.* Now, my son, I venture the prediction, that at the end of twenty years, if not sooner, the correctness of our course here will be fully and entirely acknowledged,—our vote against appointing printers to office by the President, and the effort we have made to restrain the power of the President in appointing to office without the advice and consent of the

Senate. Take care of this letter, so that you may see how the thing works with time, when you may the more fully understand my meaning.

I have very little more to say. The weather has again softened, and we have a clear sky, although the snow and ice still remain. Tell Gregory to bestir himself—to make everything move—to haul manure—maul rails—attend to the stock—give the most particular attention to the steers—and to take especial care of the corn. The horses ought now to be in good order. If "Jim" has the swelling on the shoulder still, and no prospect of its being cured soon, he had better sell him for what he can get for him. Tell Mr. Seawell to pass judgment on him. The mischievous sow ought to be put in a pen by the kitchen with her pigs; they might be raised to be fine hogs with attention. Let me know how they come on shucking corn.

Your father,
John Tyler

John Tyler to Robert Tyler

Washington
April 20, 1832

My Son:

I did not express to you all the pleasure I felt upon hearing from you, when at home, that you were employed in making yourself acquainted with the armorial bearings contained in the encyclopedia. To many persons, it would seem but a mere waste of time; but I look upon it in a very different light. There is, in truth, no study which would prove unprofitable. The person designed for a debater, either at the forum or the legislative hall, should have, in the language of Cicero, in his treatise *De Oratore,* universal information. He is thereby enabled to draw his illustrations from the remotest corners of the earth, and while he enforces, to adorn and beautify his arguments. I derived the greatest pleasure from it, because it gave me the assurance that your mind was inquisitive after knowledge, and so organized as to be capable of prosecuting its inquiries in the most rugged paths of science. This is the only way of attaining distinction and true greatness.

There are some young persons who think if they read Latin, looking into the dictionary for nearly every other word, and can repeat a few lines of poetry, they are made men. Rely upon it, that these can never rise above mediocrity. Those, on the contrary, who are deterred by no difficulties, but resolve to pry into the difficult sciences, are destined to distinction. Mr. Jefferson was a philosopher in the broadest sense, a mathematician, astronomer, etc., etc. Now, in order to accomplish all you desire, consider *time* as more valuable than money. Bonaparte, having one day visited a school, said, on departing, to the scholars: "My lads, every hour of lost time is a chance of future misfortune;" a saying which deserves to be classed among the wise sayings of the world.

You have a habit of stooping over your book as you read. This is a bad practice, and may injure your breast. You should have a table on which to rest your book, if it be heavy; and if light, hold it up well.

The House of Representatives are trying Governor Houston of Tennessee, for a breach of privilege, in beating a member of Congress in the street for what he said in the House. The Constitution declares that no member shall be *questioned* elsewhere, for what he may say in debate; and the true construction of this clause will decide Houston's fate. Large crowds attend daily, and much interest seems to be felt. The subject will occupy Congress for many weeks; and when we shall adjourn is altogether doubtful.

I have seen your cousin Maria but once. Yesterday I went to Georgetown to see her; but she had gone to Alexandria and Mt. Vernon. She is, therefore, well and happy. So tell your aunt.

Attend to the wishes of your mother, in all respects, and tell John to do so too. I hope little Alice is by this time perfectly well. I forgot to say that I have, since my return, purchased Bourienne's account of Bonaparte, with which I am much pleased, and which will afford you delight and information. It is too large to send by mail.

Tell your mother that I wrote to her last Tuesday.

With love to all,

Your father,
John Tyler

Mr. John: I recieved your letter on reaching here. You or Robert must write by every Tuesday's mail, as your mother will by Friday's. Let me know what you read, and all about the plantation. Have *hours* for reading and *minutes* for playing, and you will be a clever fellow.

Miss Elizabeth: I thank you for your pretty letter. It was written very well. You and Letitia must write me often. Learn your books and be good girls, and don't give mother occasion to scold at you.

Your father,   *J. T.*

Miss Letitia: I have just found out the way to make ice cream in the shapes: It must be frozen in another vessel, stirred with a spoon until it gets pretty thick; then emptied into the shape and set in ice. So tell your mother. A teaspoonful of flour should be sifted through muslin into it.

Father hopes that dear little Alice has got well. How are you, Miss Alice? and when are you going to write to father? Kiss Tazewell for me, and tell him to be a good boy, and not to forget me.

John Tyler to John Tyler, Jr.
Young John, not yet fifteen, was responsible for the family farmland. Although he was not at school, he would return to his studies.

Washington
Feb. 19, 1834

My Son:
I wish that you had been more particular in your last as to the extent of land covered by the farm-pen manure. I have no positive idea of the extent to which it should reach. Miller ought at once to haul the manure from the store; this he should by no means neglect, as we may not get all if he waits for the spring to come. Jo. Seawell might wish to use as much as he can get for the field at the Ordinary, if he cultivates it. Tell Miller not to be mealy-mouthed about it, but to get all he can. I am sorry that the sheep have turned out so badly. The farm is not suited to them, or they are an indifferent race. If, however, we can raise clover, we can soon improve them. I hope the clover seed have been brought home. They are at Mr. Robbins' if not at home. Had he not better borrow from Mrs. Taylor the machine with which the seed are sown at Belle-farm. It would save labor and seed. If Burwell goes for it, tell him to enquire of the seedsman all about it. It will be time to sow them next week.

I am glad to find that you have resolved to let nothing interfere with your studies; resort to other things as a recreation merely; but let your mind run on your books. That is your only chance in this life. With knowledge and information you may get along through the world after a respectable manner; but without it you can be nothing. You can learn anything at home if you apply yourself. Maria Seawell, you see, acquires a knowledge of Spanish or French without difficulty, and why not you of Latin?

Give yourself lessons in grammar and reading as if you were at school; and be sure to learn the grammar by heart. Things have taken such a turn here that I can't fix upon any day for leaving for home; but I shall pop in upon you all one of these times when you least expect me.

I hope Miller will be able to cast out some marl. Tell him that corn is rising, and to be getting it ready at all leisure times.

Your father,
J. Tyler

JAMES POLK (1845–1849)

Among the early presidents afflicted with ne'er-do-well nieces, nephews, and wards, James Polk of Tennessee was unlucky only once. Marshall Polk, his nephew and ward, seemed unable to remain at any school very long before being expelled. Each time, he confessed his errors, then begged—as in one letter—"that you will forgive the reluctance I have shown in doing that which you thought best for me," promising "that in the future I will exert myself all that I can to advance myself in my studies with as little expense as possible, and with as little trouble to you." Uncle James would forgive Marshall until the next episode.

Eventually, through presidential influence, young Marshall was appointed to a cadetship-at-large to West Point. He entered three days before the president had to write Marshall that his ailing mother had died. Whether it was school discipline or his orphaned status that spurred him, Marshall improved as a student, although his uncle regularly confessed mortification at the demerits his ward had amassed and became used to letters asking that presidential influence be employed to help some cadet friend in distress. After one scolding from the White House, Marshall insisted, "I have never neglected one lesson and have always known my tasks before entering the section-room, so you see uncle it was not my fault that I did not stand higher."

Marshall detested his schooling and especially deplored, as a Southerner, the winter gales on the bluffs of the Hudson, but he persisted through his uncle's single presidential term and beyond, writing Polk in 1849, "I am glad your term of office has expired for I used [to] think you looked troubled with the press of business which was put upon you." In 1852, he graduated and was commissioned a second lieutenant, serving in frontier operations as far away as California before resigning in 1856. When the Civil War began five years later, he joined other Tennesseans in rebellion against the Union.

James Polk to Marshall Polk

Washington City
July 3, 1848

Dear Marshall:

It is my painful duty to transmit to you the enclosed letter from *Mr. R.C. Pearson,* announcing the distressing and melancholy intelligence that your Dear Mother is no more. It appears that she died on the 23rd of Jun.— She was the best of mothers and I know the receipt of the information of her death,— will be to you a severe shock,— but I trust you will be able to bear it, with christian fortitude.— But your parents are now gone, and I shall feel a greater solicitude, if possible, for your welfare, than I have heretofore done.— D^r— Tate will no doubt write to you soon.— My advice to you is to submit to the severe affliction; with a firm reliance on an all-wise creator for aid and support in the grief which it is so natural you should feel. You must reconcile yourself to your condition,— and continue steadily to pursue your duties, at West Point.—

Your aunt requests to be remembered kindly to you. She sympathises with you, in your irreparable loss, and requests that you will write to her soon.

Your affectionate Uncle
James K Polk

James Polk to Marshall Polk

Washington City
July 24, 1848

Dear Marshall:

It has been nearly a month since I heard from you. You know that I take an interest in your welfare. I hope you will conform to all the regulations of the Academy, and perform with alacrity every duty which may be required of you. If you will do this and give regular and close attention to your studies, you have talents to enable you to maintain—not only a respectable, but a high standing in your class.— If you shall fail to maintain such a standing, it will be your own fault, and I shall be greatly mortified at it.— You should so conduct yourself as to avoid demerit marks,— and to be always prepared for your recitations.— I am frequently called upon to review the proceedings of Court Marshall in the case of Cadets,— and in almost every case, the delinquency is to be traced to culpable inattention to duty. It is a painful duty to confirm the sentence against them but the discipline of the Institution and the good of the service requires it. You must not make the mistaken calculation that because you are my nephew,— you can be protected or receive any favour. All the Cadets stand on the same footing, and if unfortunately you should offend, you must calculate to suffer the punishment which may be awarded in your case. I hope that no such case will occur; and I know that you can avoid it if you resolve to perform your whole duty faithfully.—

It is my wish that you should write to me every two weeks. If you have nothing else to communicate, you can inform me how your health is, and how you are progressing in your studies.— I shall expect to receive a letter from you once in every two weeks.—

Your Uncle
James K Polk

James Polk to Marshall Polk

Washington City
December 18, 1848

Dear Marshall:

When the official Report reached me that you had received 18 Demerit marks for the month of *October* I was greatly mortified, but did not write to you, hoping that it had been accidental, and would not occur again.— To my surprize and still greater mortification, I received to day; your conduct Report for the month of *November,* from which it appears, that instead of improving; your conduct has become worse, and that you have received 22 Demerit marks; for the latter month.— Your whole number of Demerits thus far, it seems is 60; and at that rate, you will reach before your first year expires, the maximum for which it will become necessary to dismiss you.— You can have no good excuse for such neglect of duty,— and I will say to you plainly, that as you make your bed you must lie in it. I have taken great interest in your welfare and will still do so, if you prove yourself to be worthy of it. If however you choose to disregard my wishes & remonstrances and to neglect your duty, you must . . . rely upon yourself and not on me, in future life. You may think me too strict, but in this you are mistaken. I know it is in your power to give . . . attention to your duty, to . . . the mortifying Report of your conduct which has been made for *October* and *November.* For the future I hope to receive no more such Reports.— I have great anxiety to learn the result of your examination in studies in January. It generally happens that those who have most Demerit marks, stand the [worst] examination. I hope in your case, it may be otherwise.— You should devote every moment of your time to your studies to the end that you may pass as reputable an examination as possible.— I hope for the best, but a few weeks will determine what your standing in your class is. I wrote you thus plainly for your good for you may profit by it.—Your future standing and reputation will depend upon your own conduct . . . at the Academy.—

I write this letter with pain and [word illegible]. It would give me sincere pleasure if I could write you of a different character commending you for your good conduct.— With the Report for *October* and *November* before me, this I cannot do.—

Your affectionate Uncle
James K Polk

James Polk to Marshall Polk

Washington City
January 24, 1849

Dear Marshall:

I have just examined the Official Report of the Semi-Annual examination of the Cadets—of the Military Academy, and find that you stand—in your class N° 28 in Mathematics. N° 30 [?] in English Grammar and N° 26 in "general merit."— I deem it proper to say to you, that I consider your standing respectable and I do not complain of it, though I would have been much gratified if it had been better. I hope you will be studious and attentive to all your duties; and thus secure for yourself a higher N° at the next examination.— I am satisfied that if you resolve to do so, you can obtain a better standing. The Report of your "Conduct"—for the month of December which has been made to me by the Engineer Department, represents you to have received no Demerit mks. This is a decided improvement over the preceeding month. I hope that your conduct Report for the future will prove to be free from demerits; if not a [word illegible]. Nothing is easier than to avoid them altogehter. This I learn from experience for during my whole College—I was never charged with the neglect of a single duty. The same thing, I believe was said of your father. It is only necessary that you should come to a fixed determination in your own mind, in order to avoid the Demerits altogether. I have the last Report sent to me, your whole number of Demerits since the commencement of the Academic year—60. Upon the whole I am pretty well satisfied with your progress thus far, and the remarks I have made, are made in the hope that you will see the necessity of devoting yourself with increased diligence to your studies.

I have received your letter of the 13th Instant. When the Box which was forwarded to you by Adams, & Co's Express, reaches you, you must avoid going in debt and live upon your pay. The regulations of the Academy; which prohibit a Cadet, from receiving money or any other supplies from his parents or from any other person, without special permission; are stringent and very properly so.— The articles which were forwarded to you by your aunt—would not have been sent, if it had not been apprehended, that you might not have taken a proper supply with you when you entered the Academy. Hereafter you must look to economy and under your pay support you.

Your Uncle
James K Polk

MILLARD FILLMORE (1850–1853)

Obscure as he now is, Millard Fillmore was a successful, innovative president before he became enmeshed in the conflict between his principles and his political career. States' rights and slavery also wound up splintering his party, the Whigs. An honorable and highly respected lawyer and politician in New York before succeeding to the presidency upon the death of war hero Zachary Taylor in July 1850, Fillmore had served in the Congress for six years before his election as comptroller of New York State, a position he took, despite a pay cut, to reenter politics. He had been defeated for public office only once when, in 1846, he had run for governor and the abolition question was used against him. As president, after his brief vice presidency, he was again forced to choose between his own abolitionist sentiments and his oath to uphold the Constitution. In so doing, he chose to enforce the fugitive slave laws—which finally ended his political career.

Although Fillmore's decision may have delayed the North-South divide for a few years, his Whig party was irreparably split. The letter he prepared requesting that his name not be entered as a candidate for renomination was not even read to the Whig presidential convention, and his name went forward, although he knew he could not win. He led on the first ballot and finally lost on the fifty-third. His support of public education and religious freedom, his recognizing Native Americans as citizens and having them included in the decennial census for the first time, his reestablishing the principles of the neglected Monroe Doctrine without going to war with Britain, and the expansion of trade, including the first expedition to Japan, were major achievements during his administration, but all accomplishments were submerged by the slavery issue.

A devoted family man, Fillmore frequently wrote to his children, Millard Powers (b. 1828) and Mary Abigail (b. 1832). His letters to the teenage Abigail, who was still at school when he was a vice presidential candidate, are full of gossip, affection, and fatherly concern. He sent her baskets of peaches to celebrate her successes at school, clippings from newspapers to keep her up-to-date on her father's political career, and new novels. Yet when she resolved to read no more novels, Fillmore, who thought fiction was a frivolity, was delighted. The surviving correspondence with Abigail ends just before her father's election as vice president put him a heartbeat away from the White House. One letter to her dated March 12, 1848, is an especially ironic one, since it consoles her on the death of a young friend in the usual lugubrious mid-nineteenth-century manner. The death of children then was far too common. Abigail herself died in 1858 when still a young woman, and the recently widowed Fillmore was inconsolable.

Millard Fillmore to His Daughter Mary Abigail

Buffalo, Dec. 5, 1847
Sunday, 1¼ P.M.

My Dear Daughter,

I was much gratified yesterday by the receipt of your elegantly written letter of the 1st instant. It gives me great pleasure to perceive that you improve in your penmanship; and I hope you are careful about holding your pen properly, without which you can never been an elegant and rapid writer. First learn to sit and hold your pen properly, then be careful to acquire a correct mode of forming letters, and practice will soon give ease, grace and rapidity.

You say you would like to stay there a year or less if possible, and then spend six months or a year with us at Albany—and lastly a year as a parlor boarder at some school in N.Y. or Boston.

If I find you improve your time and conduct yourself with proper discretion, as I doubt not you will, I shall be very happy to do anything for you that I can to give you a perfect education, and adorn you with every grace, that the best teachers and the best society can confer. For I love my little daughter very much, and am very anxious to gratify her in everything that is proper, presuming that she will ask for nothing else.

I sent you another copy of *Domb[e]y & Son* last night also the pamphlet signed "*Juridicus.*" What do you want of this?

We are all very busy. Mrs. Burwell has invited us to spend a few days with them, previous to our departure and we shall probably leave the house to the auctioneer tomorrow, and he will sell the furniture on Wednesday. If there are any little things you want us to bring to Albany, write in your next. I found a copy of your Newspapers which you wrote at Washington, and have packed it with my books to carry to Albany. Our court is yet in Session and that occupies all my time, week days; and therefore I can only write you on Sunday.

We have had unpleasant, sloppy weather for a few days, but it commenced snowing yesterday, and the snow is now 6 inches deep.

But I can not write more as George must carry this to the P. Office before he goes to church.

Your *Ma* joins me in love to you. We hope to see you in Albany at Christmas. That is less than 3 weeks. Will you be glad to see us? I think you will.

Your affectionate Father
Millard Fillmore

Millard Fillmore to His Daughter Mary Abigail

Albany, March 12, 1848
Sunday 8 in the Evening

My Dear Daughter,

We received yours of the 10th this evening, and your account of the death of Miss Bellows has made us feel very sad. It would not but remind us that you also are mortal, and that perhaps we have seen your last smile and heard your last adieu. But we hope not, and trust that you may be preserved to make us happy for many days to come. But death is inevitable. It may be delayed, but can not be avoided. It becomes us all therefore to live as we shall wish we had when that solemn and awful hour approaches. If we do this, we may safely trust in our Heavenly father for the rest.

I can not but feel a deep sympathy for the poor disconsolate and bereaved parents of Miss Bellows. What a terrible shock it must be to her poor old father. Little did he think when he parted with his beloved daughter in the bloom of health, that he should never see her again. And who can describe or even imagine the anguish, of her poor fond mother, who would have died to save her child, but she was not permitted to do so. Such scenes call forth the deepest sympathies of our nature, and has made your poor *Ma* feel so bad that she could not write this evening, but desired me to do so.

I do this the more cheerfully as you were so prompt in writing as I requested to let us know of your safe arrival.

We have no news here. Mr. & Mrs. Hayden left yesterday for his father's in Schondack, not to return. Your *Ma* has not been as well as usual today. We rode down to Mr. Rathbone's yesterday, and I fear she took some cold, and her throat is sorer than usual and she has remained in all day.

We had a letter from Miss Wall yesterday. She is yet at Akron teaching school, and says your aunt Mary's health is better, but that her memory fails.

We had a letter from Powers two or three days since. He was well. Mrs. Random & Daughter are yet at N.York. He with Mr. Stewart & wife returned last night.

Your *Ma* joins in love to our daughter.

Your affectionate father
Millard Fillmore

Millard Fillmore to His Daughter Mary Abigail

Albany, June 16, 1848
Friday Evg. 10 oclock

My Dear Daughter:

I received your letter some days since, but have not found time to answer it. Since my nomination much more of my time than usual is taken up by calls that I can not refuse, and by private letters that I can not neglect. I shall be most glad when the election is over, whatever may be the result. Supposing that you might desire to hear what was said by the different papers, I sent you an Evening Journal, and if you desire it, will send the weekly all the time—

Your Mother received yours of the 15th this evening. She will answer as to the article of dress. As to your studying German, I hardly know what to say. Have you books? What is the extra charge? How much time must you devote to it? I fear you will have too many studies, and will attempt too much and be a proficient in nothing. You have a good opportunity to learn Latin, and I hope you will make yourself master of it, so that you can translate for me.

How do you like your roommates? Are you pleasantly situated for the summer?

We hope to see Powers in about 2 weeks. Do you desire that he should stop at Lenox?

Your Ma and I visited Mr. Kelloggs folks at Troy last night, and staid all night—but we got little rest, and I must close and retire.

Your affectionate father
Millard Fillmore

Dear Abby   I think I will buy you some swiss muslin to make you a dress and send it to you with the bonnet and you can get it made there and the other things I will attend to   Yours affect—
Abigail Fillmore

Millard Fillmore to His Daughter Mary Abigail

Albany, Sept. 13, 1848
Weds. Evening

My Dear Daughter:

I returned here yesterday morning leaving your mother at Buffalo, & shall expect her on Saturday night. Your aunt Mary came out to Buffalo last Saturday and is staying at the Hart's. Her vital health seems much improved but yet she is very feeble. She can not stand or walk. How dreadfully she is afflicted! She suffers more or less pain all the time; and this too without hope of ever being much better. I feel very sorry for her.

Your mother took cold in going out to see her and was threatened with a kind of croup and inflammation in her lungs; but was better when I left. She is staying with Mrs. Haven. We had a pleasant time at the Fair and all passed off well.

Mr. Sheppard told me that Harriet was not married. That she was now near the foot of Lake Ontario where he had recently forwarded her your letter. He seemed to know nothing of the story that she was married in July. Strange!!

I am glad you all enjoyed the peaches so much. Your term will soon close when you will be here again. I think I shall send you to the Normal school. Every person should have some profession or trade to enable him to provide for himself. Nothing is so degrading as beggary, and nothing so painful as dependence. Learn to take care of yourself and you may avoid both.

When your mother returns she will see Mrs. Molinard about your boarding in her family and learning to talk French.

I forgot to answer your inquiry about the French History. If you will undertake certainly to read it, you may buy it, otherwise not.

We had a letter from Powers dated on the 4th—He was well.

I am too busy to say more than that I remain

Your affectionate father
Millard Fillmore

FRANKLIN PIERCE (1853–1857)

By the time Franklin Pierce was inaugurated, his only remaining child, Bennie, was dead. Bennie, to whom the Pierces were excessively devoted after the death of their other two sons, and for whose sake Pierce had agreed to accept the nomination because he wanted Bennie to be proud of his father, had been killed in early January 1853 in a railway accident. In the early years of railroads, equipment failures were responsible for many such deaths. There are no letters to Bennie in the Pierce papers. The president probably destroyed them, as he did most of his papers from the White House years. The few letters from Pierce to children precede and follow his presidency and are to his niece and nephew. In 1832, he was speaker of the New Hampshire House of Representatives and tagged as having a political future on the national level, when he wrote to his fourteen-year-old niece, Harriet Pierce, whose mother had recently died. Harriet was a student in Boston, apparently living with her aunt, Franklin's sister Betsy, when her uncle was prompted to offer seemingly motherly advice.

Following his presidency, Pierce accepted his brother Henry's son, a younger Franklin Pierce, as a substitute son and provided for his namesake's education at Andover and then at Princeton. Pierce also provided for the education of Julian Hawthorne, son of his novelist friend, who had written a campaign biography of Pierce, one of the earliest of that genre. Pierce lavished on his substitute children the affection and concern he could no longer shower on his own. Young Franklin was named his heir, and his brother Kirk received a bequest. In the aristocratic tradition, each also received a sword.

In Pierce's letters, the proverbial New England granite is tempered with generosity, affection, and concern. His interest in Franklin's successes is balanced by admonitions that he get enough rest and recreation. While concerned about the high cost of dormitory fees, Pierce is generous in paying his nephew's bills and furnishing spending money. And when the former president has to choose between making a substantial profit on a property or assisting his sister and brother-in-law, John McNeil, to educate his nieces, family loyalty wins out.

Franklin Pierce to His Niece Harriet Pierce

Pierce wrote this letter to his niece from Concord, New Hampshire, on April 1, 1832.

My Dear Niece

There is one subject I forgot to mention to you before we parted. I wish you to rise early. I don't mean very early say ½ past six for the present, but let no morning find you in bed after that hour; if you feel a little unwell when you wake let it make no difference, it would prove an excuse to which you would too often & too easily yield. I urge this upon you because it will contribute so much to your health, your spirits and your improvement. The three months now before you, Harriet, will be a period of great importance in your life. I trust it will be one of great improvement. Your health being delicate requires great care. You should by this time be well enough acquainted with your own constitution, to know, that nothing should be taken into your stomach, that is not both simple & nutritious. If you load your stomach with sweet meats et cetera you cannot be well. With a firm constitution medicine & exercise is of no avail against an ill-regulated diet. As you commence taking lessons in some of the fashionable accomplishments, you should study the graces. Whatever you do, let it be done gracefully and with ease. Observe this alike at all times and in all situations. Whether at home or [abroad] in the presence of your instructress or alone [in your room.] Among your studies neglect not that [best . . . the] Bible. Let it [be] opened before you [in the morning and] at evenin[g]

Your affect Uncle
F. Pierce

Franklin Pierce to His Nephew Franklin Pierce

Concord, N.H.
March 30, 1867

My dear Nephew—

I received your note of the 22nd inst several days since. I infer that you will require in June something more than fifty dollars but you will write two or three weeks before the close of the Term [at Princeton] and let me know definitely. When you speak of sixty *five dollars* for your room, I suppose you mean sixty five dollars for a year, not for a Term. I should regard $65 per term or session as decidedly too extravagant.

I was at Hillsboro last week. All well. Kirk is very impatient for employment and I should have gone to Boston again on his account yesterday but for the death of Major Gale whose funeral is to take place today. I shall make further explorations Monday. But the stagnation of business in all lines is such that many clerks have been thrown out of employment and it will probably be no easy task to secure a place for a new one. However I will do all I can and if unsuccessful we must turn to the next best thing, whatever it may be.—

Yr affec^t Uncle
Franklin Pierce

P.S. Have your studies enlisted your interest and have you found yourself pleasantly *at home* in the recitation room?

Franklin Pierce to His Nephew Franklin H. Pierce

Little Bows Head
North Hampton
May 24, 1868

My dear Frank.

Your letter of the 18th was forwarded from Concord and reached me here Friday. I am down Thursday and ever since a north east storm more persistent and violent than any at this season remembered by "the oldest inhabitant" has raged and is still unabated in violence—My cottage is in nice order and I have done a good deal on the acre in the way of ploughing, harrowing, p[l]anting and sitting out 150 trees shrubs & vines.

I think [you] will enjoy a week or more *with* me during your vacation.

Your class rank shows that you have worked reasonably hard and with satisfactory success. Kirk seems to be doing very well. But *mere* impulse is too prominent in his nature and is the thing which he ought to guard against and habitually suppress. His hopefulness and sanguine temperament has always led him to give too little time to the exercise of patient thought and calm judgment. He is a capital young man and has ability enough. But his letters altho' they evince good findings and good sense, show, also in the matter of grammar & spelling, that he has not used his advantages as he should have done, which would have made him perfect at least in both of these very essential matters in every line of life. If he had more patience and less impulse he could make up in the next three months out of snatches of time at his command, these *essentials* now lacking and to me mortifying—

He should never write a letter, even to you or me or his father without knowing that every sentence is correct in grammar and every word correctly spelt.

I said a word or two to him two or more times upon this subject and as he has never alluded to it in reply, I have ceased to repeat my suggestions, but in a letter written to him today remarked that he need not write to me often and that there was no occasion for him to write in a *hurry*—I feel the deepest interest in him and am as he has reason to know ready to do what I can to ensure his success and happiness. I shall only ask that he take upon himself the discipline and do the things without which he can scarcely expect to attain either.

Yr. affect. Uncle
Franklin Pierce

Franklin Pierce to His Nephew Franklin H. Pierce

Concord
May 25, 1869

My dear Frank—

I received yesterday your note of the 20th. I have been upon my land all day and am now too tired to say much in reply. I regret your disappointment with regard to your grade in the class. I feel it too, more or less personally. It is, however, really of little consequence. I have no doubt that you have done your best; and with that conviction I am satisfied and you ought to be. If your letter implies that you have fallen to 27th in your class it has been a pretty awful fall and would lower my ideas of your capacity. However continue to do your best and no result will seriously trouble me whatever it may be. The power of acquisition is a very small part of a man's powers so far as success in after life is concerned. I thought I should attend the commencement of your graduation, but it is now not likely that I shall do so—you have done your best—. That satisfies me. Continue to do it.

My letters from Kirk are very satisfactory—

I am not disturbed by your disappointment. I have done what pleased me and you have done your best. It would be very unreasonable for either of us to indulge any disagreeable thought about anything unavoidable.

When you are at home and at the sea side with me we can talk the whole [thing] over.

I suppose from your letter that you now want no more money. If you do write me at once—

Yr. affect. Uncle
Franklin Pierce

I am too weary to read what I have written but trust you to make out the meaning—I hope to see you well and strong in July—

JAMES BUCHANAN (1857–1861)

The only bachelor president, James Buchanan, had his era's usual bounty of official and informal wards, among them his nephew James Buchanan Henry and his niece Harriet Lane. Young James was seven when his father died, and Buchanan became his guardian. The boy was moved into Buchanan's spacious country home, Wheatland, near Lancaster, Pennsylvania. Some letters to both children are written from there, where Buchanan, between political appointments and after his presidency, lived like a country squire.

In the Senate with only modest presidential ambitions, and then as an ambassador abroad or in the Cabinet, Buchanan was away in Washington or across the Atlantic when James Henry was at school, first in the little Moravian town of Lititz nearby. "He required me," Henry remembered in the 1880s, "to write to him once every month with great exactitude, and to each boyish letter he would write a prompt reply, carefully but kindly criticizing every part of it; and if I had been careless in either penmanship or spelling, he would give me sharp reproof, which coming from the hero of my youthful worship, made an impression which I remember to this day." But few of these letters survive.

Harriet Lane was also about seven when her mother, another Buchanan sister, died in 1839, leaving four orphans. Harriet was the youngest. Rather than raise her in a bachelor establishment, Buchanan placed her in the home of two maiden ladies, the Misses Crawford. When she was old enough for female boarding schools, he sent her first to Virginia and then to a convent school in Georgetown, although neither he nor his niece were Roman Catholic. Although he was nearby in Washington, he wrote her letters of exhortation, admonishment, and moral uplift. When she began maturing into a beautiful young lady of independent ideas, he increased the moral pitch of his letters. When he became president, having remained a bachelor, she became his White House hostess, which she was when he entertained Queen Victoria's eighteen-year-old son, the Prince of Wales, in 1860. Since diplomatic niceties required that he write, before and after the visit of the future Edward VII, to the boy's mother, there are no letters from the last of the aristocratic presidents to a boy Prince of Wales.

James Buchanan to James B. Henry

Wheatland
[Lancaster, Pa.]
17 August 1849

My dear James,

Yours of the 10th Instant went first to the Bedford Springs & was returned to the place. I left the Springs on the 28 ultimo & passed a few days at Mercersburg & in its vicinity on my way home. There were many inquiries about you there, to all of which I answered that although you had made but poor progress in your education considering your opportunities; yet that you now gave promise of doing much better. I trust you may be able to enter the Sophomore Class at Princeton. Should you fail in this, I shall be most grievously disappointed. Indeed I should then nearly abandon all hope of your doing any good in any of the learned professions.

I do not wish you to have any plugs put in your teeth by any dentist at West Chester. After your vacation, when we go on to Princeton, I can get Dr. Gardette to plug your teeth. Your plugs have already cost so much, that I now wish them to be well done.

Mr. Greenhow his three daughters, and a nurse have been staying with us for some time: but I believe they will go home next week. Harriet is still here; but seems so anxious to be in Town that probably she may not remain long. Eldridge Lane is still with me. I shall be delighted to see you at your vacation *should you answer my reasonable expectations:* otherwise your presence will afford me no pleasure.

Yours affectionately
James Buchanan

James Buchanan to Harriet Lane

Wheatland, January 17, 1851.

My Dear Harriet:—

I have received yours of the 15th, and we are all happy to learn that you have reached Washington so pleasantly. I hope that your visit may prove agreeable; and that you may return home self-satisfied with all that may transpire during your absence. Keep your eyes about you in the gay scenes through which you are destined to pass, and take care to do nothing and say nothing of which you may cause to repent. Above all be on your guard against flattery; and should you receive it, "let it pass into one ear gracefully and out at the other." Many a clever girl has been spoiled for the useful purposes of life, and rendered unhappy by a winter's gaiety in Washington. I know, however, that Mrs. Pleasanton will take good care of you and prevent you from running into any extravagance. Still it is necessary that, with the blessing of Providence, you should take care of yourself.

I attended the festival in Philadelphia, on the occasion of the arrival of the steamer "City of Glasgow," but did not see Lilly Macalester. Her father thinks of taking her to the World's Fair in London. I saw Mrs. Plitt for a moment, who inquired kindly after you.

We are moving on here in the old way, and I have no news of any interest to communicate to you. Eskridge was out here last night, and said they were all well in town. I met Mrs. Baker yesterday on the street with her inseparable companion. She was looking very well.

I have not yet determined whether I shall visit Washington during the present session; but it is probable that I may, on or about the first of February.

Give my love to Laura and Clementina, and remember me in the kindest terms to Mr. and Mrs. Pleasanton.

Miss Hetty and James desire their love to you.

Yours affectionately,
JAMES BUCHANAN.

James Buchanan to Miss Maria B. Weaver
Maria Weaver was Buchanan's grandniece, child of his sister Maria's daughter Jessie. Jessie had married a jobless young man for whom Buchanan, then secretary of state, found a clerkship in his department, getting him $800 a year more than anyone else who had served less than ten years by securing equivalent raises for anyone in a position to complain. By the time the letter to young Maria was written, Buchanan was no longer president, Lincoln having succeeded him in 1861.

The Jessie referred to is not Buchanan's niece, but another of her daughters.

Wheatland, near Lancaster
April 11, 1862

My dear Maria,

I am pleased to have received your favor of the 7th Instant & that it is so well & correctly written & spelled. I observe but one word incorrectly spelled & strange to say that it is *niece*. You spell it *"neice."*

I am sorry to learn that you have not been going to school since last spring. I hope you have been wisely occupying your time & instructing yourself. With whom do you and your youngest brother live at Darnestown? I thought he had been with the Misses Quincy at Washington.—I would thank you to inform me how old you are.

I occasionally hear of Jessie through Mr. Baldwin at Washington who is the agent of Lieutenant & Mrs. Magaw. She has had great advantages & as I am informed has improved them well. She speaks several modern languages. I trust you will not suffer her to surpass you in solid accomplishment—in truth, in good sense, in virtues & pure sentiment & in heartfelt piety.

My health, thank God! is good considering my age. I shall be seventy-one should I live until the 23rd of this month. We lead a quiet & tranquil life here although we keep quite engaged of company to prevent it from being dull.

Miss Hollis has not been well for some months, though she is not so sick as to confine her much of the time in bed. Miss Lane is well. She spent three months of the winter with Mrs. Roosevelt in New York. They both desire to be kindly remembered to you.

Yours affectionately,
James Buchanan

P.S. As I receive my letters free you need not put a stamp on yours to me.

James Buchanan to Miss Maria B. Weaver
Buchanan had managed to push his grandniece into attending school by offering to pay the bills.

Wheatland, near Lancaster
September 23, 1862

My dear Maria,

I have received your two letters of August & September & am always gratified to hear from you. As the time is approaching when you will become an inmate of Fair Hill Boarding School I enclose a letter to Mr. Kirk with a check on the Chemical Bank of New York for $50. By the terms I perceive that I need only pay in advance $43.34, but you may want some little things in the beginning. Whilst I desire you to be economical I do not wish to deprive you of any of the books, accessories or comforts which other girls may enjoy in the school. Please do write to me as soon as you are fixed there.

I am happy to perceive that every word in your late letters is correctly spelled. In your previous letter you wrote "Presbyter*e*an" for Presbyterian, "Ba*b*tist" for Baptist, "sep*e*rated" for separated, "twelth" for twelfth, leaving off the f. I am sorry to learn that Jessie's English has been neglected. To be able to speak & write our native tongue correctly is the most important branch of education. This you will, no doubt, speedily accomplish. Indeed, from your limited opportunities, I am agreeably surprised that you write so well. Be a good & courteous girl.

With my kind regards to your father I remain yours affectionately,

James Buchanan

CHAPTER TWO

The Democratized Presidency, 1861–1901

Even before the first shots were fired, the immense impact of the Civil War changed the nature of the American presidency. Almost an accidental president because of the prewar fragmentation of political parties, Abraham Lincoln, the little-known choice of a minority of the electorate, was the first of the new breed. He was as different from most of his predecessors in origin and outlook as would be the new constituencies of young people through whom one can observe the shift in perception of the presidency. Presidential letters would become more avuncular than fatherly, and letters *to* the presidents—a markedly new development—show that the public recognized that the occupants of the White House had become more approachable. The daughter of the Marquis de Lafayette could write to George Washington; the daughter of a laborer could write to President Lincoln or Harrison or Cleveland and expect to receive an authentic response. The political exploitation of such presidential letters to children would await yet another metamorphosis in the office.

We find in the letters even of forgettable presidents of these years a private integrity and charm that the public record, focused upon the sleazy politics of what Mark Twain called the Gilded Age, fails to notice. A letter from James Garfield tells his sons not to gloat over his nomination to the presidency. Rutherford B. Hayes, amid the turmoil over his disputed election in 1876, tells his son Ruddy to be "very guarded in speech. If Mr Tilden is elected all good citizens will quietly acquiesce, and will wish to give him and his administration fair play. If we are successful, it will not be handsome behavior for any of my family to exhibit exultation or to talk boastingly, or be vain about it." The Lincolnesque statement of democratic principles was hardly to be bettered, but Hayes is now hardly remembered.

ABRAHAM LINCOLN (1861–1865)

Because Lincoln was not a national figure until 1858, catapulted to prominence by the debates with Stephen A. Douglas, there is little evidence of pre-presidential interest in him by young people. A few messages in children's "confession," or autograph, albums remain—and there is the unforgettable letter to Grace Bedell, reproduced here. It is curious that the best-known correspondence between president and child occurred before Lincoln was actually president, or had even been elected. The eleven-year-old Miss Bedell had written to the candidate about the advisability of his growing a beard in October 1860, several weeks before the election.

Just after, according to a contemporary account, Lincoln was at a celebration of his victory in Chicago when a little girl timidly approached him. She wanted his autograph, she confessed. Lincoln looked behind her and saw a problem: "But here are other little girls," he said; "they would feel badly if I should give my name only to you." The girl admitted that they were eight in all. "Then," said Lincoln, "get me eights sheets of paper, a pen and ink, and I will see what I can do for you." The materials were brought, and Lincoln sat down in the crowded drawing room and penned a sentence, and his signature, on each sheet. Each little girl carried off her own personal message from the president-elect. So goes the story, which appears in J. G. Holland's *The Life of Abraham Lincoln,* published only a year after Lincoln's death. But none of the eight sheets have turned up.

A wartime president, beset by more troubles than any chief executive before him, Lincoln had little time as president for the small talk of juvenile correspondence, especially after putting his signature on dozens, sometimes hundreds, of commissions, pardons, stays of execution, and civilian passes to cross enemy lines. He appears to have seldom written to his own children, or at least little such evidence has surfaced, other than a few brusque one-line notes and telegrams to his eldest son, Robert. Of his four sons, one died before Lincoln reached the White House, one died in the White House, and the sickly Thomas (or Tad), for whom Lincoln acknowledged a gift of white rabbits in 1862, barely survived his father.

Perhaps because of the memorable letter to Grace Bedell, or fed by the many pardons he issued for the confused and underage recruits in the Union army whose infractions of discipline had left their lives in jeopardy, the myth of Lincoln's rapport with young people has grown to proportions that the facts fail to support. The last known letter from Lincoln to a child was written in February 1864, more than a year before his assassination in April 1865.

Abraham Lincoln to Miss Rosa Haggard
The "confession" or autograph album was a popular Victorian-era possession. When Lincoln was staying at a hotel in Winchester, Illinois, where he was to deliver a speech, the daughter of the proprietor brought him her album in which to write a message. The doggerel advice prompted the proprietor's other daughter, Linnie, to bring her album to Lincoln two days later, but the result was less than half as long and even less inspired. Only the lines to Rosa Haggard appear here.

> To Rosa—
>> You are young, and I am older;
>> You are hopeful, I am not—
>> Enjoy life, ere it grow colder—
>> Pluck the roses ere they rot.
>
>> Teach your beau to heed the lay—
>> That sunshine soon is lost in shade—
>> That *now's* as good as any day—
>> To take thee, Rosa, ere she fade.
>
> Winchester, Sep. 28. 1858.   A. Lincoln—

Abraham Lincoln to Miss Mary Delahay
Mary was the daughter to Lincoln's friend Mark W. Delahay, in whose home Lincoln was staying while in Leavenworth, Kansas. On the day of his departure for Springfield, Illinois, Mary brought him her album in which to inscribe a message.

December 7, 1859

Dear Mary
   With pleasure I write my name in your Album. Ere long some younger man will be more happy to confer *his* name upon *you*.
   Dont allow it, Mary, until fully assured that he is worthy of the happiness. Dec. 7– 1859   Your friend
                              A. Lincoln

Abraham Lincoln to Miss Grace Bedell

                                                                        N Y

Hon A B Lincoln   *Westfield Chatauque Co*
      Dear Sir   *Oct 15. 1860*

    My father has just [arrived] home from the fair and brought home your picture and Mr. Hamlin's. I am a little girl only eleven years old, but want you should be President of the United States very much so I hope you wont think me very bold to write to such a great man as you are. Have you any little girls about as large as I am if so give them my love and tell her to write to me if you cannot answer this letter. I have got 4 brother's and part of them will vote for you any way and if you will let your whiskers grow I will try and get the rest of them to vote for you   you would look a great deal better for your face is so thin. All the ladies like whiskers and they would tease their husband's to vote for you and then you would be President. My father is a going to vote for you and if I was a man I would vote for you to[o] but I will try and get every one to vote for you that I can   I think that rail fence around your picture makes it look very pretty   I have got a little baby sister she is nine weeks old and and is just as cunning as can be. When you direct your letter dir[e]ct to Grade Bedell Westfield Chatauque County New York
    I must not write any more   answer this letter right off   Good bye
                                                  Grace Bedell

                                    Private

Miss Grace Bedell   *Springfield, Ills.*
My dear little Miss.   *Oct 19. 1860*

    Your very agreeable letter of the 15th. is received.

    I regret the necessity of saying I have no daughters. I have three sons—one seventeen, one nine, and one seven, years of age. They, with their mother, constitute my whole family.

    As to the whiskers, having never worn any, do you not think people would call it a piece of silly affection if I were to begin it now? Your very sincere well-wisher
                                                  A. Lincoln

Abraham Lincoln to Michael Crock

Although Michael Crock, of 860 North Fourth Street, Philadelphia, was addressed by Lincoln as "My dear Sir," no one by that name has been identified in Philadelphia records, and his letter does not survive among the Lincoln Papers, which gives rise to the supposition that Michael was indeed a child. The very nature of his gift to Tad Lincoln, which the president acknowledges, also suggests a juvenile gift giver.

Executive Mansion
April 2, 1862

My dear Sir

Allow me to thank you in behalf of my little son for your present of White Rabbits. He is very much pleased with them.

Yours truly
Abraham Lincoln

Abraham Lincoln to Miss Fanny McCullough

Lt. Col. William McCullough of the 4th Illinois Cavalry was killed in a night encounter near Coffeeville, Mississippi, on December 5, 1862. Before the war, he had been clerk of the McLean County Circuit Court at Bloomington and had professional associations with Lincoln in that capacity.

Executive Mansion,
Washington, December 23, 1862.

Dear Fanny

It is with deep grief that I learn of the death of your kind and brave Father; and, especially, that it is affecting your young heart beyond what is common in such cases. In this sad world of ours, sorrow comes to all; and, to the young, it comes with bitterest agony, because it takes them unawares. The older have learned to ever expect it. I am anxious to afford some alleviation of your present distress. Perfect relief is not possible, except with time. You can not now realize that you will ever feel better. Is not this so? And yet it is a mistake. You are sure to be happy again. To know this, which is certainly true, will make you somewhat less miserable now. I have had experience enough to know what I say; and you need only to believe it, to feel better at once. The memory of your dear Father, instead of an agony, will yet be a sad sweet feeling in your heart, of a purer, and holier sort than you have known before.

Please present my kind regards to your afflicted mother.

Your sincere friend
A. Lincoln

Abraham Lincoln to Master Willie Smith
Willie Smith, a boy of twelve, admired Lincoln greatly. A friend of his father told Lincoln, which resulted in this response.

Executive Mansion, Washington

Master Willie Smith: February 23, 1864

    Your friend, Leroy C. Driggs, tells me you are a very earnest friend of mine, for which please allow me to thank you. You and those of your age are to take charge of this country when we older ones shall have gone; and I am glad to learn that you already take so lively an interest in what just now so deeply concerns us. Yours truly,

A. Lincoln

ANDREW JOHNSON (1865–1869)

If Andrew Johnson's letters to his children evidence failings in spelling and in grammar which may have appalled the children themselves, it was not for want of his trying. A tailor's apprentice with no formal schooling, he worked hard and prospered in his trade, and then turned to politics in his adopted state of Tennessee. Having been taught to read and write by his wife, Eliza McCardle, whom he married when he was eighteen, he cautiously dabbled in politics, moving from local to state affairs, serving two unremarkable terms as governor before he manipulated his election to the Senate. There he was a lonely figure among Southern Democrats in speaking out to preserve the Union. When war began, he was the only senator from the South who chose to remain in his seat. His reward for loyalty came when Lincoln wanted to run for reelection on a unity ticket in 1864. By then military governor of subdued Tennessee, Johnson became vice president and, five weeks later, via an assassin's bullets, president.

    Although the spelling falters and the punctuation flags, Johnson's letters to his children show his ardor for education. To his teenage daughter Mary, he argues that education should have a higher priority than "bacon and cabbage" and urges that she learn how to "write a good hand" and acquire composition skills. He remains concerned about the education of his sons, especially when one leaves school because an alleged outbreak of cholera in the area had convinced him "that he could learn as much at home."

    Andrew, Jr., born in 1852, was his youngest child of five. As ex-president, retired to Tennessee, Johnson confided to Andrew, in sending him stamps for his collection, that Greeneville was indeed "a dull place." Johnson's political rise had begun there. After his narrow escape from conviction by a vindictive Senate after his trumped-up impeachment, and his failure to be renominated, he still longed, in spelling and grammar that remained faulty, for the Washington that had rejected him. Bereft of his White House secretaries, the ex-president's writing mechanics as a private citizen no longer had the polish of his public messages.

Andrew Johnson to His Daughter Mary
Johnson's younger daughter, Mary, was a student in the Rogersville Female Academy in Tennessee. Miss Mary T. Davidson and "Miss Virginia" were classmates.

Washington City   Dec 7th 1850

My dear daughter,

Your very welcom letter of the 23d ultimo has just come to hand— I assure you it was a source of no ordinary pleasure to me to hear that you were so well pleased with the School, hoping that you will be as well satisfied at the termination of the session as you are at the begining. As to the Small matter of eating you can do with any kind of fair for a while— It will only prepare you for better living hereafter. I am also gratified to find that the teachers pay you so much attention— Miss Davidson is the young lady you heard me talking about having tra[v]eled with from Abingdon to Marion. She is an orphan girl and deserves much credit for the manner in which She has improved and conducted herself. In a few yers if She lives She will make a woman of the first order of intellect. If you think proper you may tender to her my best respects— I presume that She will remember me very distinctly— I See you have dated your letter Greeneville instead of Rogersville, this little thing shows the force of habit— If I were in your place I would habit my self to writing a hand Some heavier than you do and write frequent— Learn how to write a good hand and good composition—. I most Sincerely Sympathise with the young lady expeled from School, yet there must be government and subordination and those that will not submit to the regulations of the institution must suffer the penality— A young lady hardly ever recover from a blow of this kind, hence the importance of duly considering well what they do that comes in conflict with the prescribed rules for the government of the School— A young lady that will not be controlled there will not be any where else—

I hope that Miss Virginia is restored to good health before this time.— you must give them my best respects— I have nothing new of interest to write at this time— The city is very dull so far— It has been raining here the last six days without intermission, there must a general rise in all the water courses. I suppose Robert is now about getting ready to Start for Franklin College— I received a letter from him the other day the only letter I received from home since leaving except yours— I hope you will write to me often this winter—

My dear child you have reached that tim of life which enables you to see the great advantages of educating and qualifying yourself for usefulness in this life.— Never mind the bacon and cabbage[.] there are ma[n]y human beings who think they are living sumptiously if they onely have plenty of good bacon and cabbage— I hope you will devote your Self to study and profit by your advantages— You must write to your brother Robert frequently this winter and during his absence— There is but four of you and you must cherish respect and love for each other— In School sustain yourself as honorable and highminded—be guilty of no low and vulgar acts or expressions even with your associates, for there is the place to make a good character and to induce others to form a high opinion of you— When you see a young lady indulge in things of the kind even with her intermit [intimate] friends it causes you to forme a bad opinion of her— Let your bearing be dignified and chaste with your closest friend— There is one other thing I will suggest and that is—in making up your acquaintance among strangers, be careful who you make intermit friends—have but few if any secret keepers or in other words have no secrets to keep. To day persons are friendly to morrow they burst into as many pieces as a touchmenot— The true policy is to be friendly with all and too friendly with none— Infine so demean yourself as to command the love and respect of all teachers and pupils and the censure and ill will of none— Your devoted father,
      A. Johnson

Andrew Johnson to His Son Robert

Nashville Tennessee
April 16th 1854

My dear Son,
  I received your last note informing me that all were well at home, which is an item of news that is always welcom with me— I hope you and your brother are progressing with your studies as rapidly as the nature of the case will permit, for it is all that you and him will have to rely upon in the future,

is your professions— Our little family have no ancestral honors to rely on nor fortunes to Sustain her, hence the importance of the more effort on our part— But the family who lays its own foundation has much more to be proud of than the one that is content with merly living upon that of those who have gone before them— You and your broth[er] have it in your power to do much more than your father has ever done, for you and him can now add your own efforts to what little he has done, which will be some advantage I will not say how much; but Something— It is not because you and Charles are my children that I make the following remark but because it is true— You and him have talents enough, nature has done her part if you will but do yours— Nothing great can be accomplished without effort and application— Solomon's remarks on the conduct of the sluggard and that lethargy which hangs about too many young men like the night mare, should be read by all young men at least once a week— The effort should be constantly making while health permits, prompt, present and efficient *action* Should [be] his motto, instead of lasitude, inertness and procrastination— now not the future—to day, not to morrow— Postponement and delay are the feelings and the arguments of the dull, Stupid and dreary *Sluggard*— Let the foundation of your moral standard be, Justice, prudence, temperence, virtue, self reliance and fortitude; which is the foundation of all genuine religions; a religion that does not embrace these as its leading eliments is not of divine origin, and has no connexion with the only true and living divinity, the great source and centre of all good— It was not my intention Sunday morning as it is, when I sit down to write a homily on morals or any other Subject but merly to let the family know that I had been disappointed in starting for home this morning as I designed to do, which would have enabled me to reach home on Wednesdey no accidents happening—I fear now that I will not be able to leave before Thursdy the 20th the day I expected to be at home— The East Tennessee & Georgia Rail Road Company have made application for one fourth of the bonds to be issued by the State to aid in the construction of the Bridge at Loudon on the Tennessee River— Mr Crozier being away at Jackson who you will remember is required by law to Sign the coupons which prevents the issuance of the bonds till his return which will be on tuesday or wednesdy next—but I intend to start as soon as he comes and the bonds are executed and hope to be at home on this day week and eat dinner with the family that day—

There is no news of much interest that occurs to me now— The weather to day is cold and raining almost approaching a Sleet—the fruit in this region of country is all killed by the late frosts— I hope there is no danger of Pattersons being beat by that little contemptabl bundle of self conceit and importance— I have received a letter from Milligan in which he seems not to like his defeat very well and talks as though he was willing to try Taylor again in the next contest— I have secured for Milligan the agency of the Bank for that entire district to the extent of the suspended debte which is close upon $140,000 and will yeald him a handsom profit if managed properly— I have appointed R. G. Payne commissioner of Internal Improvements— he will commence opperations soon and no doubt will expose Some of their numerous frauds that they have been practicing on the State— Old man White and Hays so far get along very well— Hays told me the other day that he had been better satisfied since White commenced than at a[n]y former period of time— One of Mr White's daughters [will] mary on tuesday next, the name of the man not remembered at this moment— The understanding is that she does well—

Tell Mr Harold to be sure and have my coat done for I Shall need it as soon as I get there— I hope all the articles forwarded home will reach there before I do, there will be time for them to be there if they go through directly— I have brought a basket and some other little notions for your little brothe[r] and a little chair for Liz & Florence &c—

        Your father Andrew Johnson

Andrew Johnson to Andrew Johnson Jr.

        Greeneville Tenn
        May 11th 1869

My dear son

Enclosed you will find an envelope with three French stamps which you will place with your collection of curiosities of this kind—

The letter which is written in french you will translate into English against [the time when] I come up to see you, which will be in a few days— This will be a very good way to keep your french fresh in your memory. You ought to make yourself a good Scholar as you can if you will only make the effort to do so— A few hours every day will do [a] great deal in the course of a year and followed up will accomplish the desired in a shorter period than you now suppose—

You must have your hooks and lines in good condition by the time I come up as I want [to] have one more fishing frollic before I go hence—

Belle forgot to take her painting when she was here, let it be sent up soon and placed somewhere in the parlor—

There is not much news here to communicate, Greeneville is a dull place and seems likely to continue so— The country is much more interesting than a lifeless village as Greenevill[e] is at this time—

> *Accept assurances [of] a*
> *father's sincere affection—*
> Andrew Johnson

ULYSSES S. GRANT (1869–1877)

As soldier, farmer, and unsuccessful businessman—Ulysses Grant's three careers before the war returned him to military life—the future president used his pockets as his filing cabinets. He wrote little and kept few papers. But for his military records, which were carefully organized (as he was a professional soldier by training and had a corps of adjutants), he admitted that "the only place I ever found in my life to put a paper so as to find it again was either in a side coat-pocket or the hands of a secretary more careful than myself." As a colonel of Volunteers and afterward as a general, he wrote few letters that were unrelated to his army duties. After the war, he felt that he deserved a token of appreciation from the American people—the presidency. In the White House, he did as little and delegated as much as was possible, looking on the office as his reward rather than his responsibility.

Grant's nonmilitary correspondence reflects his unconcern with administration on any level. Few letters to children, even his own, survive—none, it seems, from the White House. Writing was a labor for Grant, and the wit in his mock commission for the young son of an officer in his command is a rarity. Although Grant mastered quickly the laconic style of correspondence used by the military, it was only late in life that he managed to write with fluency and ease. Then, as ex-president, while he was dying of throat cancer, he wrote his *Personal Memoirs* in hopes of paying his debts and securing his family's finances. It was an unexpected and deserved success.

Ulysses S. Grant to Master Willie S. Hillyer
Willie was the young son of Capt. William S. Hillyer.

Head Quarters Distruct South East Mo.
Cairo, Nov 1st 1861

TO ALL WHOM IT MAY CONCERN
By virtue of the authority in me vested I do nominate and appoint
                    Master Willie S. Hillyer
Pony Aid de Camp with the rank of major to be attached to my staff. All stable boys will take due notice and obey him accordingly
—Done at Cairo this Novr 1, 1861
                    U. S. GRANT
                    Brig. Gen. U.S.A.

Attest
Jno. A. Rawlins
Assistant Adj General

Ulysses S. Grant to His Daughter Nell

Headquarters Armies of the United States
Cold Harbor Va. June 4th 1864

My Dear little Nelly,

I received your pretty letter more than a week ago. You do not know how happy it made me feel to see how well my little girl not yet nine years old could write. I expect by the end of the year you and Buck will be able to speak German and then I will have to buy you those nice gold watches I promised. I see in the papers, and also from Mama's letter, that you have been representing "the old woman that lived in a Shoe" at the Fair! I know you must have enjoyed it very much. You must send me one of your photographs at the Fair.

We have been fighting now for thirty days and have every prospect of still more fighting to do before we get into Richmond. When we do get there I shall go home to see you and Ma, Fred, Buck and Jess. I expect Jess rides Little Rebel every day! I think when I go home I will get a little buggy to work Rebel in so that you and Jess can ride about the country during vacation. Tell Ma to let Fred learn French as soon as she thinks he is able to study it. It will be a great help to him when he goes to West Point. You must send this letter to Ma to read because I will not write to her today. Kiss Ma, Cousin Louisa and all the young ladies for Pa. Be a good little girl as you have always been, study your lessons and you will be contented and happy.

                    From
                    Papa

Ulysses S. Grant to His Son Ulysses, Jr.
When Grant took office in 1869, he was, at forty-six, the youngest man to serve as president and had a young family. In 1870, his teenage son, "Buck," became a plebe at West Point. Willie Cole was the son of Sen. Cornelius Cole of California; Dent Casey was Grant's nephew via the family of Mrs. Grant, who had been Julia Dent. Fred was Grant's eldest son.

Washington D.C. Oct. 23d 1870

Dear Buck,

Without anything special to say, but supposing that you are always glad to hear from home, I write you. By this time you must be over all your hardships, and well settled down to your studies. I hope you are doing well, and, above all, are contented. I should like to hear what mark you get in your studies, and how it compares with the class generally. Fred has been doing quite well this year. He has, I think, gone up a section in all his studies, except in Engineering, and two sections in that with the prospect of going up still another. He is up to his limit in demerit however— Your Ma is now very uneasy. Yesterday Jesse, Willie Cole and Dent Casey went off, we suppose to Capt. Ammens, and have not yet returned. You know your Ma is always alarmed if her children are out of sight for any length of time.

Let us hear from you often. Make it a point to write to Jesse and Nellie alternate weeks, and to your Ma each week.

Yours Affectionately
U. S. Grant

RUTHERFORD B. HAYES (1877–1881)

A lesser Civil War general, Ohio congressman, and governor, Rutherford B. Hayes was the victor in the closest presidential election since Aaron Burr and Thomas Jefferson campaigned to an electoral vote tie in 1800. In popular votes, Hayes trailed the Democratic candidate, New York governor Samuel B. Tilden. As a letter dated November 8, 1876, from Hayes to his son Birchard, confides, he was sure he had lost the election and intended to take his defeat in good grace. Yet a Republican-dominated special electoral commission determining where the disputed electoral votes of several Reconstruction-corrupt Southern states should go decided on party lines and gave the election to Hayes.

As president, Hayes removed Union occupation troops from the old Confederacy. Otherwise, he was prudent and cautious, even announcing, to free his hand from political pressure, that he would not run for reelection. He returned to Spiegel Grove, in Fremont, Ohio, content with his administration and willing to watch further events from afar. That caution can be seen in his advice to a boy, Frank Richter, in 1881, to leave politics to his seniors, and to his eldest son a decade earlier to avoid overexertion and excitement even in playing baseball.

When the Hayes family moved to the White House, the elder sons, Birchard and Webb, were already twenty-three and twenty-one. Rud, just eighteen, was a Cornell freshman, and Fanny (Frances) and Scott were nine and six. When Fanny went off to a girls' school in Cleveland, Hayes wrote to her regularly and tutored her in writing. Once, complaining about her punctuation, he added, "But your letter is so good and has so few [other] faults that on the whole I must compliment you on its excellence." He was affectionate but stern with his sons, advising them to avoid cards, billiards, drink, and tobacco, and to cultivate "the wee small courtesies of life." Unlike many presidential children, they lived unflamboyant and successful lives.

Rutherford B. Hayes to Birchard Hayes

Columbus [Ohio]
June 3, 1870

My dear Boy:
—I see by the *Journal* you are playing baseball and that you play well. I am pleased with this. I like to have my boys enjoy and practice all athletic sports and games, especially riding, rowing, hunting, and ball playing. But I am a little afraid, from [what] Uncle says, that overexertion and excitement in playing baseball will injure your hearing. Now, you are old enough to judge of this and to regulate your conduct accordingly. If you find there is any injury you ought to resolve to play only for a limited time—say an hour or an hour and a half on the same day.

Uncle and Sarah [Jane Grant, visiting Columbus] with our whole family are well. We had General Sherman at our house Wednesday evening with a pleasant party.

Sincerely,
R. B. Hayes

Rutherford B. Hayes to His Son Rutherford Platt Hayes

Columbus, O[hio]
8 Nov 1876

My Dear R[uddy]:

You will naturally wish to know how we feel since the defeat. Scott Russell is rejoiced because now we can remain in Columbus where the cousins and friends live, and will not have to go away off to Washington, which he evidently thinks is a very bad place. Fanny shares in this feeling, but has a suspicion that something desirable has been lost. Birch and Webb dont altogether like it, but are cheerful and philosophical about it. Your mother and I have not been disappointed in the result however much we would prefer it to have been otherwise. The hard times with the cry of reform against a party long in power, it has seemed to me would carry the day, from the very first. We escape a heavy responsibility, such labors, great anxiety and care, and a world of obliging by the defeat. We are now free and independent, and at peace with all the world, and "the rest of mankind."

It would have been a great gratification to try to establish Civil Service reform, and to do a good work for the South. But it is decreed otherwise and I bow cheerfully to the result.—Birch will go to Cambridge in a day or two. Webb will remain here for the present.

We are all well. You will talk discreetly, and exhibit no ill temper about adversaries. The less said about the matter by you, the more sure you will be to make no mistake—

Sincerely

R. B. Hayes

Rutherford B. Hayes to His Son Rutherford Platt Hayes

Columbus, O[hio]
3 Dec 1876

My Dear R[uddy]:

We are all in usual health. The winter has set in. Snow enough for poor sleighing is on the ground. Fan and Scott with a new sled are enjoying the streets with hosts of other little folks.

Our Thanksgiving dinner we took at Lauras with all of the kindred here. The crowd of children enjoyed themselves noisily and made the scene lively.

It is probable that by the time this reaches you, or within a day or two afterwards, the result of the election will be known. In either event it is proper that you should be very guarded in speech. If Mr. Tilden is elected all good citizens will quietly acquiesce, and will wish to give him and his administration fair play. If we are successful, it will not be handsome behavior for any of my family to exhibit exultation or to talk boastingly, or be vain about it. There are many reasons why success may be a calamity to us personally. Defeat will be in many ways preferable. However it is, be quiet and good tempered about it.———Write to us often. Give full particulars of your teachers, friends, studies and amusements.

With love to you from all of the household

Affectionately
H.

Rutherford B. Hayes to Frank P. Richter

Fremont [Ohio]
April —, 1881

My young Friend:

—Leave politics to your seniors. Try to fit yourself to be a useful man and a good citizen. Don't be lazy. Be truthful and industrious. Learn to support yourself. Study the history of your country, and always remember that to make others happy will make you happy.

Sincerely,

R. B. Hayes

JAMES A. GARFIELD (1881)

James A. Garfield emerged from the war as a young major general and, like many other Union officers, turned to active politics. In 1880, when Hayes declined to run again, Garfield, then an Ohio congressman, had just been elected to the Senate. Hopelessly divided between Maine senator James G. Blaine and former President Grant, seeking a third term, the Republican national convention turned to the new Ohio senator on the thirty-sixth ballot. His elder children were mature enough to understand the implications of his sudden national prominence, and Garfield wrote often to Harry and James—sixteen and fourteen, and both at St Paul's School in New Hampshire—to keep them aware of election issues, as well as to discuss their translations of Sallust and Homer. Even earlier, while in Congress, Garfield had written to them regularly while traveling, educating them about the places he saw and urging them to follow his progress on a map. Only urgent letters on family business failed to include some history or geography.

Just one letter to his children from his few months of the presidency survives—a letter of little interest but its date, for on July 2, 1881, less than two weeks later, after Garfield had returned from his summer cottage at Long Branch, New Jersey, he was shot by a frustrated and demented office seeker who claimed that he was a follower of Grant. The president lingered for eighty days in a hopeless condition, unable to perform any presidential act but the signing of an unimportant paper, while Congress and the Cabinet pondered problems of disability and succession. Meanwhile, his youngest son, Abram, only eight, remained on the family farm at Mentor, Ohio, once writing in a very childish hand that he was sorry his father was hurt and giving him news of their dog, old Veto. On September 19, 1881, Garfield, who had experienced only four active months in the presidential office, died.

James Garfield to His Sons Harry and James

GRAND HOTEL
San Francisco, Cal
May 7, 1875

My Dear Children—
In my letter of yesterday to Mamma, I told you of my visit to Mr. Ralstons on Saturday & Sunday last, and of my visit to the mint on Monday. Since I sent that letter off, I have received Mamma's and Harry's letter of the 28th April. I see that all of your letters are stamped at the Washington Office at 8 P.M. so that if you put them in the office by six P.M. they will come right on the same evening. It takes them eight days to reach me. I am very thankful to you for your good letters. They keep me from getting homesick—and I want you all to know that the oftener you write me, the happier I am. I promised in this letter to tell you of my visit to the Chinese.

On Tuesday afternoon Mr. Sargent took us to the Court House where we got the chief of police and a Chinese interpreter—& with them we spent three hours visiting what is called the Chinese Quarter. Soon after the discovery of gold in California in 1848, the Chinese began to come over here. At first a few came in junks—and afterwards they came in American ships until now there are about 150,000 of them scattered up and down this Coast from Oregon down to the Mexican line, and back in the mountains among the mines. About half of all that number are now in this city—and they all live in one portion of the City occupying only six or seven blocks. Though you will see them at work everywhere in the city, yet they go home nights to their quarters. In the first place, we went to their places of worship, which they call Joss Houses. Joss is their name for god—and they believe in a great many gods—and worship their images. Hence they are idolaters. They believe in good gods and in evil ones—and seem to care more about appeasing the evil than worshiping the good. Their Joss Houses are full of very curious things: images of their gods—bronze figures of lions and dragons warriors & queens—and lamps are kept burning day and night before the images. The walls of the Joss Houses are covered with strange figures, Chinese writings & pictures—and one of the lions they pretend to feed every day to keep him from hurting them. When I was there, there was a piece of pork in his mouth—Isn't it strange that anybody should be afraid of a bronze lion? From there, we went into the houses where the Chinamen live. You have probably some Chinamen in Washington. They all wear wooden shoes, and a frock of blue jean, made like a man's shirt which comes down nearly to their knees. They shave their heads close except a large circular patch on the top & rear of their heads, and that they grow its full length—and braid it up into [a] queue—which hangs down behind almost to the ground. Most of their rooms are so small that you would not think that it was large enough for a pig. They take a room as large as mamma's bedroom, & put up scaffoldings about the size of a berth in a sleeping car and twenty would cook and sleep in them. I was in one not very large house—where there were 500 Chinamen living in the two upper stories. Some of them have six or seven bricks set up on a box, and a little fire built in the bricks was their only means of cooking. Out on a little roof—the size of that over my library—they would have shanties built and a dozen Chinamen lived in them. Their principal food is rice and fat pork—and little ducks which are found in China and pressed flat & preserved in oil—& sent over here. When one of their number dies, they put his body in a box and put lime on it, and when a few months later there is nothing but bones left, they pack them into as small a box as they can, and ship them back to China to be buried. They are great smokers but they smoke opium instead of tobacco, and it makes them go to sleep very easy. Some of their houses and kitchens were so nasty that [it] almost made me vomit to go through them—but there were some nice, clean places. We went into a Chinese restaurant and had them make us a cup of tea, which was very good. Their mode of making it was to put the tea leaves into a cup, and pour hot water in it, & put another cup over it, and then in a few minutes we drank it off, & they filled the cup again with hot water.

In the evening Gov. McCook & I went to Mr. Ralston's house here in the city to dine; and then we went to the theatre with Mrs. Ralston & Miss Leland—and saw Mrs. Bowers play Mary Queen of Scots.

On Wednesday, Mr. Sargent, and Gen Burns of the Army, took us out on a little steamer to look at the bay. We stopped at Alcatraz Island where the U.S. have a long fort—and then we went to Angel Island where there are several companies of soldiers.

From the deck of the steamer, we could look out through the strait which is called the "Golden Gate"—and see the Pacific Ocean. On Angel Island, I climbed to the top of a high hill where I got a good view of the bay and the City. I don't know that you can find all these places on the map, but I think you can some of them.

I should have told you that they won't take paper money here in the stores; they only take gold and silver. When I first came here, I had to buy some coin—I gave a man $40 in greenbacks and he gave me $34.80 in coin. In the bank you will see bags full of eagles & double eagles—look in your arithmetics and see what they are. The miners bring down what they call dust, and it is melted up into bars, & then at the mint, it is made into coin. Give my love to mamma, & grandma—and Aunt Carrie & all the little ones. You know how anxious I am to have you good children & to have good reports from you.

Affectionately your Papa
J A Garfield

James A. Garfield to His Sons Harry and James

Mentor, Ohio
October 31, 1880

My Dear Boys—

This is the first time for many weeks when we have no visitors; and I take a few moments to write. I suppose Mamma and Mollie have kept you informed of the course of affairs here, during the last fortnight—You have also seen from the Daily Tribune something of what I have been saying—I take this occasion, just on the Eve of the Election to call your attention to some of the peculiar phases of the contest. During the months of June and July, the *leaders* of the Democratic party discussed questions of public policy; and none but the lowest class of orators and Editors descended to personal abuse—But when they say that the people were afraid to trust the financial & business interests in the hands of the "Solid South," & that the fair discussion of the merits of the two parties was hurting their chances—they began a personal warfare upon me that has hardly been Equalled for violence and malignity in our history. Among other things they insisted & published Everywhere, that I did not enjoy the confidence and support of my friends and neighbors—This was handsomely answered by the fact that the 19th Dist gave a Republican majority of more than 12,600—being an increase of 1606 above the majority which Gov. Foster received last year—

The failure of the Democrats to capture Ohio, and their loss of Indiana, made them unusually desperate—and hence to their other attacks they have added the forgery of a letter on the Chinese question—which they still insist is genuine. I think that many intelligent and honest Democrats will hesitate to support a party which uses such means to secure a victory—As the case now stands, I think the Republican chances of success are good. There would be no doubt of it, were it not for the very large foreign vote of New York City—But our friends there are quite confident of success—So far as I am concerned, I have not allowed myself to become so absorbed in the contest, as to lose sight of the great array of forces against us—Nor have I at all set my heart upon success as necessary to my usefulness and happiness—I want you to know that I neither sought nor wished the nomination—On many accounts, I would have preferred to go into the Senate, and Enjoy the freedom of study and debate—But now that I am nominated & have borne in silence the abuse and falsehoods of the campaign I shall be glad to be successful—I have replied to no slander except the forgery—In the nature of the case, no one else could reply but me; & you have seen my letter—When this reaches you the Election will be in progress; and a few hours later, the result will be know[n]. I know that you will both feel a deep interest in the outcome—but I have learned to trust your discretion, & so have no fears that you will be unduly cast down if I am defeated, nor that you will do or say anything unseemly if I am Elected—You have by inheritance and Education so much of the Equipoise and prudence from mother, that I have long ago, ceased to have much anxiety about you—so far as discretion of speech and action about family affairs are concerned—Above all, Dear Boys, whatever shall happen, I beg you to keep on the Even tenor of your way, holding up, with Even a little more than usual vigor and steadiness to your work—It would make me very proud to know that during the first week of November 1880, my boys marked a little higher in studies, decorum, punctuality and industry than in any previous week of the term—and that they were in no wise thrown off their balance by this Presidential Election—The Family are all well, though a little tired out by the crowds of visitors. "Veto" is growing in size Experience and discretion. Hal's colt is doing well—having nearly recovered from a few scratches received by running into the fence wire—The Alderney calf has been sold for $100—& taken to Illinois—but two younger ones, of purer breed have come from Baltimore—The back yard, side yards & part of the front yard have been turfed—The Entrance to the wood-shed has been Enclosed for winter—The new steam Engine has come—and is soon to be in its place under a lean-to soon to be Erected on the East End of the old Engine house—The huskers are busy in the corn—The buckwheat will be threshed before the week Ends—and we will greet you with Indian pudding and buckwheat cakes when you come for the holdiays—Five loads of apples have gone to the cider mill—& twelve barrels of cider are fermenting on the northside of the office. Judd has gone home to Michigan to vote; and if our two pilgrims were here there would be no absentees—& none present but the family & Mrs. Brown—This, in brief is the situation on the Eve of the battle—The whole house-hold join me in tenderest love to you both—And now, my brave lads, Good night—

As Ever Your Papa
J. A. Garfield

Abram Garfield to President and Mrs. Garfield

Mentor Ohio
July 10th 1881

My Dear Papa and Mamma

I am very sorry that you were hurt.

I heard that you were going away and I am glad of it but I want to know where you are going are you Coming here? Old Veto is a very good dog now he has not growled at me nor any body else since I have Been here.

I am glad that I am not there because I would only be in the way.

I suppose you will not have time to write to me. Give my love to all.

Abram Garfield

CHESTER ALAN ARTHUR (1881–1885)

After news of Garfield's death reached New York, young Alan Arthur stood beside his father, Chester Alan Arthur, as he took the oath of office. Alan was beginning his freshman year at Columbia. He and his younger sister, Ellen, were being brought up by their father. Nell Arthur, their mother, had died of pneumonia in January 1880. At home with them, Arthur was kindly but stern, insisting that his son address him as "Sir." He also saw to it that Alan was dapperly dressed—as, always, was Arthur—and that he learned sailing and horsemanship. During an outing at Cooperstown just before Arthur became vice president, a newspaperman reported watching the portly and fashionably attired candidate take time out to watch his son play baseball. At about the same time, Arthur, who doted on his son, gave him a family heirloom watch. The note describing it appears to be the only letter to a child that survived the destruction of Arthur's papers that followed his departure from the White House.

Chester Alan Arthur was as unlikely a person to succeed to the presidency as has appeared in American history. Long associated with the New York patronage machine controlled by state Republican boss (and senator) Roscoe Conkling, he had become collector of customs for the port of New York—the apogee of spoils system abuses—in 1871. A covert reason to nominate him as vice president had been to give the customs job to another party loyalist. Propelled to the White House on Garfield's death, Arthur surprised detractors who knew his history. He pushed for civil service reform and ran a clean if unremarkable administration. Knowing late in 1884 that he was incurably ill, he made little effort to run for reelection, although he permitted his name to be placed in nomination. He lost to perennial candidate James G. Blaine, who then lost to Grover Cleveland. In brief retirement in New York, he burned most of his papers.

Chester Alan Arthur to C. Alan Arthur

> *Alan:*—
> Keep the enclosed letter, so you will remember that Dr. Herndon has your grandfather's watch chain during his life.
> It then belongs to you with the watch, which is at Tiffany's.
> *Dec 1880*   CAA

Note on envelope:

Alán (accent on last syllable to rhyme with man) is my father, whose maternal grandfather was the naval hero Wm. Lewis Herndon. There is a monument to him at Annapolis.

CAA

GROVER CLEVELAND (1885–1889, 1893–1897)

While governor of New York, Grover Cleveland would walk each day from his residence in Albany to his offices in the Capitol, greeting each child he passed with a "Hello, little one!" Sometimes the children would echo the greeting to the stout bachelor governor, who was amused by the "little one" tag unceremoniously reapplied to himself. Most of his letters to children, which emanated from the White House by the dozens while he was president, resulted from his marriage, in 1886, when he was forty-nine, to Frances Folsom, his ward of twenty-one who had just graduated from Wells College in New York. It was his second year in office. A White House wedding and the youth of the first lady magnetized young people, who wrote to the couple in Washington and on their much-publicized travels and holidays. But almost all the letters were answered by the young Mrs. Cleveland, who responded to letters from children both to her husband and to her, most of them from teenage girls.

After Cleveland began a young family of daughters during his four years between nonconsecutive terms (the only president with such interrupted service), his sympathies with young writers seem to have increased. Still, his office responded brusquely to such letters, and he brushed off a student request in 1890 to speak to a class, saying, "I have too many other things to do." One of the few letters to a youngster that has survived postdated his presidency by several years. In it, Cleveland offered his nephew Fred Bacon instructions on how to write a letter. Cleveland had warmed by then. Ten years out of the White House, the ex-president was still receiving mail from children and still responding to them.

Grover Cleveland to a Little Girl Named Mollie
Cleveland was still a bachelor president at the time of this letter and had little experience with small children. He married later in the year.

Washington
March 18, 1886

My dear little girl:

I thought my birthday would be a pretty dull affair, and I didn't suppose that anyone would care enough about such a dreadfully old man to notice the occasion. But when I read the nice little message in which you sent, with your mother's, 'compliments and love,' I began to think that birthdays were pretty good things after all.

I shall enjoy the roses very much. They are nicer than any I am in the habit of seeing or smelling. And then you know in such cases a great deal depends on the way you get flowers and the person from whom you receive them. I hope, Mollie, that in the years to come and when you are a pretty old girl, all the flowers which are given you will bring to you as much pleasure as I enjoyed through this morning's floral gift.

Grover Cleveland

Grover Cleveland to Master George Allen Bennett

Stuart, Florida
March 30, 1906

My dear little friend:

I am very glad you wrote me a letter of congratulation and good wishes on my birthday. And I thank you for kindly thinking of me. We ought to be very good friends, if we were born on the same day of the month, though there is a difference of sixty years in our ages. The years seem to pass much more quickly, as a person grows older and when you arrive at the age of sixty-nine, as I have done, you will wonder at the short distance between nine and sixty-nine.

I think the 18th of March is the best day in all the year to be born on and I hope you do too. I wish for you a great many Happy Brithdays, and that as each one passes, there will be such increase in your mental and moral growth and such improvement in every way that you will be insured a life of honor and usefulness.

Your friend
GROVER CLEVELAND.

BENJAMIN HARRISON (1889–1893)

The president between Cleveland's two terms was the grandson of "Old Tippecanoe," the ninth President. Benjamin Harrison of Indiana was the last of the young Civil War generals to reach the White House. He had written often to his own small children from the fronts, telling them of his dreams for the future. As the war was drawing to a close early in 1865, he urged Russell Harrison, then ten, and Mamie, then seven,

> to help Ma fix up the yard, and keep . . . all nice and clean. The grape vines will need to be tied up and trimmed and the strawberry bed weeded and thinned. . . . You know that I want to see our little house and everything about as neat and trim as an old maid.
>
> What a good time we will have when we all get together again at home, and Pa does not have to go away to war any more. We will make everything about the dear cottage shine like a new dollar, and will try to keep things as bright inside the house as they are outside. We will have the stable fixed up and bring our horse . . . home and maybe get a nice little buggy to ride in.

If a horse and buggy were his symbols of success, they came soon. Known as "Administrative Ben" for his exactitude as an officer, Harrison was equally strict and able as a civilian, rising from court reporter to public prosecutor, prosperous lawyer in practice, unsuccessful candidate for governor but successful candidate for senator. His children were grown by the time he defeated Cleveland in a "front porch" noncampaign (he seldom left Indianapolis) and became president. He was already a grandfather, and his presidential and post-presidential correspondence to young people was largely, although not all, to his grandchildren. One letter to a child he saw only once is remarkable for its sensitivity and for its revelation of the more relaxed standard of presidential security in practice in the more leisurely nineteenth century, despite a recent assassination. What child could now innocently enter the presidential compartment of a train or other conveyance to take the president by surprise and proffer a gift? Four-year-old Elizabeth Llida Jones was able to do that in 1889 and later received a letter on Executive Mansion letterhead and a doll from the grandfatherly Harrison. Today there would be neither letter nor doll, for little Elizabeth would have been turned away by the omnipresent Secret Service.

Benjamin Harrison to Miss Elizabeth Llida Jones

Late in the 1880s, postmaster general and department store magnate John Wanamaker presented Carrie Harrison, the wife of the president, with an elegant French doll, complete with a luxurious wardrobe from which Mrs. Harrison was to choose gowns to be made up for her. On visiting Richmond, Indiana (the president was from Indianapolis), President and Mrs. Harrison discovered a greeting party of one in their Pullman car, Elizabeth Llida Jones, who presented the full-bearded former Civil War general with a gift of a penknife and a kiss, and then scurried away. The president reciprocated with a letter and a gift of his own—the Jumeau doll.

Executive Mansion
Washington
Dec. 23d, 1889

My dear little friend

When you came into my car at Richmond I did not see you until you stood at my feet, looking up to me so sweetly, that I did not know but [that] a little fairy had come up through the window. But when I picked you up and you gave me a kiss, then I knew it was a real little girl. The pretty knife you handed me I will keep till you are a big girl and when I go back to Indiana to live you must come to see me, and I will show you that I have not forgotten you.

The little doll which you will find in the box with this letter is for you, and I hope you will think it is pretty. If the doll could talk she would tell you how much I love to be loved by little children.

Affectionately yours,
Benj Harrison

Benjamin Harrison to His Grandson Benjamin Harrison

Executive Mansion
Washington
June 22, 1890

Dear Ben,

Why didn't you write Grandpa a letter yesterday, so it would come to him today. I know you were playing in the sand all day and didn't think of your lonesome old "Dampa" once. I wish I had you to sit on my desk and put the rubber bands all in the big inkstands—but I expect you have something that pleases you better down at Cape May—and if you will write me a good letter and tell me all about what you and "Maywee" do every day then I won't bring you back to this hot old town. Did you leave that bad, black imp that used to get on your back here, at the White House, or did he get on cars and go to Cape May with you. I haven't seen him about here—and if he's here, he must eat down in the kitchen, for he didn't come to the table with me. I don't know where he sleeps, for he wasn't in your bed. If he didn't go on the cars with you, maybe he has started to walk down to Cape May, and you had better keep a watch for him, and not let him get in the house.

Suppose you have Charlie catch him if he comes on the porch and take him out in the big sea and drown him.

Kiss Sister Mary for Grandpa and don't let that bad boy get on your back.

Your loving Grandpa
Benj Harrison

WILLIAM McKINLEY (1897–1901)

A small-town Ohio boy who became an officer in the Union army and afterward a lawyer and politician, William McKinley was the epitome of moral rectitude in an age when small-town values dominated American life. The Cleveland kingmaker and financier who sponsored him might have been known as "Boss Hanna," but the label never affected the buoyant confidence possessed by the voting public that McKinley stood for everything simple and good in American life. To his young nephew and ward, James McKinley, he once wrote, "Look after your diet and living, take no intoxicants, indulge in no immoral practices. Keep your life and your speech both clean, and be brave." The president practiced what he preached.

The McKinleys had no children who lived to maturity, and the president doted on his nieces and nephews and kept in touch with them by mail. In a period when few children would have thought of writing to a president, he replied to Mary Woodward's suggestions during the war with Spain about what to do with the Philippines, Cuba, and Puerto Rico that he was pleased by her "intelligent interest in these grave public matters," to Minnie Wagner about White House visiting arrangements, and to John Dempsey that he was glad to see "that although so young you have begun to take an interest in public affairs."

His problems with his teenage nephews began when they caught the prevailing war fever and, despite their youth, wanted to enlist. In response to a telegram from the White House, young Jim McKinley came over for dinner, after which he asked the president whether he and his cousin, Jim Barber, might join the 8th Ohio Volunteers. Of Jim, McKinley wrote to Col. C. V. Hard of the 8th, "He is a good boy. I am very fond of him and have the deepest interest in him. He is . . . possibly rather young for a soldier; still I can but admire his patriotism and so send him to your regiment for enlistment. I hope he will make a good soldier." He did, and eventually earned a commission. Jim Barber joined too, and was killed in action.

After the war, McKinley rode his crest of popularity into a second term but served only a few months of it. In Buffalo, New York, on September 6, 1901, to speak at the Pan-American Exposition, he was shot by an anarchist gunman. He died eight days later.

William McKinley to Master John Dempsey

May 24, 1897

Dear Master John,
I was pleased to receive your letter dated the seventeenth instant and to know that although so young you have begun to take an interest in public affairs.
This should be the case with all bright young Americans.
Very truly yours,
William McKinley

William McKinley to James McKinley

March 1, 1898

Dear James:
I got your letter some time ago; was glad to hear from you. I presume by this time that Ida is at home with her baby and you are all enjoying her visit.
The incidents connected with the school I noted in the papers. I am glad that everything was so happily ended. You must not let any little difference with teachers interfere with your industry and studiousness. I am sure you have the ability to make up before Commencement any lessons you have failed in during the year. This I would do under all circumstances. A little more work each day and it will be accomplished. In after life you will always be glad that you did it and you know how much pleasure it will give me to

learn that you have done it. You know I have a deep interest in your welfare and just now is a very important time in your life. Just get up your grit and go in and make up for all that is lost and graduate in June. This will make us very proud of you.

With love to all,

Your affectionate Uncle,
William McKinley

William McKinley to George S. Barber

April 23, 1901

Dear George:

I have your letter of to-day. I am sorry you want to go into the army. My judgment would be that you would make a mistake to do it. You are doing well where you are, and will do still better. You are better off now in income than though you were a lieutenant in the army, with opportunities for increasing your income which you would not get as an officer. Of course you know I would be willing to do anything you might want me to, especially if I thought it was for your good; and I would not advise you, as you know, except for your own good. If John goes into the navy that is as much of a contribution as I think your family ought to make, especially inasmuch as poor Jim lost his life in the service. I do not know what you mother may say when she writes you, but I feel quite sure from a little talk I had with her when at home that she would be very unhappy if you went into the army. Think it all over again and see if you do not come to the conclusion that you had better let well enough alone.

Your Aunt Ida joins me in love to you and John.

Affectionately yours,
William McKinley

CHAPTER THREE

The "Bully Pulpit" Presidency, 1901–1953

The term "bully pulpit" is Teddy Roosevelt's; however, the pulpit itself was one that his predecessor, William McKinley, had no idea he had created as a result of the Spanish-American War of 1898, which pushed the United States into the outside world. An America emerging from a far-flung conflict, with postwar colonies extending to the far rim of the Pacific, was a different nation than the inward-looking one created by the Civil War.

Using the powers he had inherited to enlarge the scope of his office, Theodore Roosevelt set a pattern for the more ambitious of his successors by exploiting the presidency as pulpit and as pivot for change. The occupant of the White House could now use his signature, if he wanted to, on letters official or informal, to make statements on larger issues than the actual addressee warranted. Exploiting the simplicity of language appropriate to a young audience, a presidential letter could deal with public issues in easily understandable terms, and with a broader audience than one young recipient in mind—since presidential letters (other than within the family) seldom now remained private. Parents of a child receiving a presidential letter in the new century would rush it to a local newspaper if the White House did not release it first.

A master of that approach was Woodrow Wilson, whose father had been a Presbyterian minister in Staunton, Virginia, and who recognized that the White House was the chief pulpit in the land. Presidential letters to young people were still fatherly in the most self-revealing ways, as with Theodore Roosevelt and Calvin Coolidge, and avuncular in the classic older fashion, as with Herbert Hoover and Harry Truman. But with Franklin Roosevelt came mass communication by radio, and a new distance despite the new intimacy created by his voice being heard in millions of homes. By the time Harry Truman's second term crossed into the second half of the century, even newer media, and newer promotional uses even for such traditional media as the lowly letter, created unanticipated barriers to intimacy.

THEODORE ROOSEVELT (1901–1909)

The youngest president in the nation's history at the time of his accession on McKinley's death, Theodore Roosevelt in September 1901 was only forty-three. His eldest daughter, Alice (b. 1884), was the child of his first marriage. His second marriage resulted in Theodore, Jr. (b. 1887), Kermit (b. 1890), Ethel (b. 1891), Archibald (b. 1894), and Quentin (b. 1897), and in filling the White House with children—his own and their friends. Whenever he was separated from them by presidential travel, or they were away from Washington, he would keep them affectionately informed. He sometimes sent the younger ones, who were barely able to read, what he called "picture letters," although the pictures show that his enthusiasm for drawing was greater than his artistic talent. Since other children came to play at the White House in this far more relaxed era of security, they were not immune from presidential messages either, nor from presidential scoldings—as when both Quentin and his friend Charlie Taft were caught applying spitballs to the staid portraits of former presidents.

Young enough and vigorous enough to think of himself as almost a playmate of his children and their friends, the president wrote to them as if he were their age, romped with them in the old barn at Sagamore Hill on Long Island, the Roosevelt home, and had pillow fights with them in the White House. The presidential menagerie is a regular subject of their letters—cats, dogs, guinea pigs, and other domestic creatures that TR not only tolerated but enjoyed. Beyond the fun-and-games level, the older children were growing into young adulthood, and their father filled his letters to them with loving exhortations about books, public affairs, education, and their possible careers, sometimes apologizing for writing in a "preaching vein."

When out of the White House after two strenuous terms, Roosevelt, still a rather young elder statesman, retained an interest in young people, and—both in and out of the family—they appear in his correspondence almost to the end of his life in 1919.

Theodore Roosevelt to Sarah Schuyler Butler

TR sent "picture letters" not only to his youngest children, but also to other youngsters. Sarah Butler, daughter of Nicholas Murray Butler, soon to be president of Columbia University, had sent her father's friend a note congratulating him on his first birthday in the White House.

White House
Nov. 3rd, 1901

Dear little Miss Sarah,

I liked your birthday note *very* much; and my children say I should draw you two pictures in return.

We have a large blue macaw—Quentin calls him a polly-parrot—who lives in the greenhouse, and is very friendly, but makes queer noises. He eats bread, potatoes, and coffee grains.

The children have a very cunning pony. He is a little pet, like a dog, but he plays tricks on them when they ride him.

He bucked Ethel over his head the other day.

Your father will tell you that these are pictures of the UNPOLISHED STONE PERIOD.

Give my love to your mother.

Your father's friend,
THEODORE ROOSEVELT.

Theodore Roosevelt to James A. Garfield

Jimmy Garfield, named for his assassinated grandfather, was the son of lawyer James H. Garfield, who became Roosevelt's secretary of the interior. The letter thanks "Jimmikins" for a Christmas present and describes how Christmas was observed in the TR White House.

White House, Dec. 26, 1902.

JIMMIKINS:

Among all the presents I got I don't think there was one I appreciated more than yours; for I was brought up to admire and respect your grandfather, and I have a very great fondness and esteem for your father. It always seems to me as if you children were being brought up the way that mine are. Yesterday Archie got among his presents a small rifle from me and a pair of riding-boots from his mother. He won't be able to use the rifle until next summer, but he has gone off very happy in the riding boots for a ride on the calico pony Algonquin, the one you rode the other day. Yesterday morning at a quarter of seven all the children were up and dressed and began to hammer at the door of their mother's and my room, in which their six stockings, all bulging out with queer angles and rotundities, were hanging from the fireplace. So their mother and I got up, shut the window, lit the fire, taking down the stockings, of course, put on our wrappers and prepared to admit the children. But first there was a surprise for me, also for their good mother, for Archie had a little Christmas tree of his own which he had rigged up with the help of one of the carpenters in a big closet; and we all had to look at the tree and each of us got a present off of it. There was also one present each for Jack the dog, Tom Quartz the kitten, and Algonquin the pony, whom Archie would no more think of neglecting than I would neglect his brothers and sisters. Then all the children came into our bed and there they opened their stockings. Afterwards we got dressed and took breakfast, and then all went into the library, where each child had a table set for his bigger presents. Quentin had a perfectly delightful electric railroad, which had been rigged up for him by one of his friends, the White House electrician, who has been very good to all the children. Then Ted and I, with General Wood and Mr. Bob Ferguson, who was a lieutenant in my regiment, went for a three hours' ride; and all of us, including all the children, took lunch at the house with the children's aunt, Mrs. Captain Cowles—Archie and Quentin having their lunch at a little table with their cousin Sheffield. Late in the afternoon I played at single stick with General Wood and Mr. Ferguson. I am going to get your father to come on and try it soon. We have to try to hit as light as possible, but sometimes we hit hard, and to-day I have a bump over one eye and a swollen wrist. Then all our family and kinsfolk and Senator and Mrs.

Lodge's family and kinsfolk had our Christmas dinner at the White House, and afterwards danced in the East Room, closing up with the Virginia Reel.

Your father's friend,
Theodore Roosevelt

Theodore Roosevelt to His Son Kermit
Kermit was sixteen when he first read a Charles Dickens novel, and he asked for his father's opinion of it and of what novels ought to do for the reader. Frederick Selous was an English big-game hunter admired by TR. Selous, who wrote popular books about his African adventures, died in action against the Germans in East Africa in 1917.

The White House, Washington.
November 19, 1905

Dear Kermit:

I sympathize with every word you say in your letter, about Nicholas Nickleby, and about novels generally. Normally I only care for a novel if the ending is good, and I quite agree with you that if the hero has to die he ought to die worthily and nobly, so that our sorrow at the tragedy shall be tempered with the joy and pride one always feels when a man does his duty well and bravely. There is quite enough sorrow and shame and suffering and baseness in real life, and there is no need for meeting it unnecessarily in fiction. As Police Commissioner it was my duty to deal with all kinds of squalid misery and hideous and unspeakable infamy, and I should have been worse than a coward if I had shrunk from doing what was necessary; but there would have been no use whatever in my reading novels detailing all this misery and squalor and crime, or at least in reading them as a steady thing. Now and then there is a powerful but sad story which really is interesting and which really does good; but normally the books which do good and the books which healthy people find interesting are those which are not in the least of the sugar-candy variety, but which while portraying foulness and suffering when they must be portrayed, yet have a joyous as well as a noble side.

We have had a very mild and open fall. I have played tennis a good deal, the French Ambassador being now quite a steady playmate, as he and I play about alike; and I have ridden with Mother a great deal. Last Monday when Mother had gone to New York I had Selous, the great African hunter, to spend the day and night. He is a perfect old dear; just as simple and natural as can be and very interesting. I took him, with Bob Bacon, Gifford Pinchot, Ambassador Meyer and Jim Garfield, for a good scramble and climb in the afternoon, and they all came to dinner afterwards. Before we came down to dinner I got him to spend three quarters of an hour telling delightfully exciting lion and hyena stories to Ethel, Archie and Quentin. He told them most vividly and so enthralled the little boys that the next evening I had to tell them a large number myself.

To-day is Quentin's birthday and he loved his gifts, perhaps most of all the weest, cunningest live pig you ever saw, presented him by [Oscar] Straus. Phil Stewart and his wife and boy, Wolcott (who is Archie's age) spent a couple of nights here. One afternoon we had hide-and-go-seek, bringing down Mr. Garfield and the Garfield boys, and Archie turning up with the entire football team, who took a day off for the special purpose. We had obstacle races, hide-and-go-seek, blind man's buff, and everything else; and there were times when I felt that there was a prefect shoal of small boys bursting in every direction up and down stairs and through and over every conceivable object.

Mother and I still walk around the grounds every day after breakfast. The gardens, of course, are very, very disheveled now, the snap-dragons holding out better than any other flowers.

Your loving father,
T.R.

Theodore Roosevelt to His Daughter Ethel Carow Roosevelt

Washington
June 24, 1906

Darling Ethel:
Mother is torn by conflicting emotions—regret at leaving me and longing to see all of you. She is too cunning and pretty for anything, and seems at the moment to be really well and enjoys the rides that we take almost every afternoon. She has just disciplined me with deserved severity. Except when the weather forbids we breakfast and lunch on the portico and take dinner on the west terrace, which is really lovely. This afternoon we spent an hour sitting under the apple tree by the fountain.

You will love Audrey; but I do not want Mother to ride her until you have thoroughly tried her, for gentle though she is, she is a high-spirited mare, and if she has not had much exercise will kick and buck a little from mere playfulness.

Tell Archie that the other day as Mother and I were driving out to the horses we passed a large pile of fine sand on Sixteenth Street. There were several boys on it, two of them already buried up to their waists, while the others were industriously shoveling the sand still higher around them. The two bowed with eager friendliness, and then we saw that they were the Newberry twins.

Today as I was marching to church, with Sloan some twenty-five yards behind, I suddenly saw two terriers racing to attack a kitten which was walking down the sidewalk. I bounced forward with my umbrella, and after some active work put to flight the dogs while Sloan captured the kitten, which was a friendly, helpless little thing, evidently too well accustomed to being taken care of to know how to shift for itself. I inquired of all the bystanders and of people on the neighboring porches to know if they knew who owned it; but as they all disclaimed, with many grins, any knowledge of it, I marched ahead with it in my arms for about a half a block. Then I saw a very nice colored woman and little colored girl looking out of the window of a small house with on the door a dressmaker's advertisement, and I turned and walked up the steps and asked them if they did not want the kitten. They said they did, and the little girl welcomed it lovingly; so I felt I had gotten it a home and continued toward church.

I am concerned to hear that Phil got into a scrape and was bounced from St. Marks. I hope it is only temporary. I am very sorry to learn that poor Jack is still having hard work with his studies. It is not his fault at all.

There is nothing in Kermit's school record to have warranted him in trying to compress the last two years in one. Has the lordly Ted turned up yet? Is his loving sister able, unassisted, to reduce the size of his head, or does she need any assistance from her male parent?

Your affectionate father,

The Tyrant.

chorus of Offspring (led by daughter)
"For he is a tyrant king!"

Theodore Roosevelt to His Son Archibald Bulloch Roosevelt

Washington
April 11, 1908

Dearest Archie:

Ethel has bought on trial an eight-months' bulldog pup. He is very cunning, very friendly, and wriggles all over in a frantic desire to be petted.

Quentin really seems to be getting on pretty well with his baseball. In each of the last two games he made a base hit and a run. I have just had to give him and three of his associates a dressing down—one of the three being Charlie Taft. Yesterday afternoon was rainy, and the four of them played five hours inside the White House. They were very boisterous and were all the time on the verge of mischief, and finally they made spitballs and deliberately put them on the portraits. I did not discover it until after dinner, and then pulled Quentin out of bed and had him take them all off the portraits, and this morning required him to bring in the three other culprits before me. I explained to them that they had acted like boors; that it would have been a disgrace to have behaved so in any gentleman's house, but that it was a double disgrace in the house of the Nation; that Quentin could have no friend to see him, and the other three could not come inside the White House, until I felt that a sufficient time had elapsed to serve as a punishment. They were four very sheepish small boys when I got thru with them!

Your loving father

Theodore Roosevelt to Miss Marjorie Sterrett

TR was a militant ex-president when, early in World War I, a Brooklyn thirteen-year-old, Marjorie Sterrett, had sent a dime to the editor of the New York *Tribune* with the hope that it would inaugurate a fund for the building of a battleship to be called the *America*. TR became an early contributor, but sufficient funds never materialized. The Cornelius Roosevelt mentioned was the third child of Theodore, Jr., born on October 23, 1915.

Oyster Bay [New York]
February 5, 1916

Dear little Miss Marjorie,

On behalf of my four grandchildren I join in the effort to help you and your schoolfellows put our country in shape to "Fear God, and Take Her Own Part."

I enclose a dollar. Forty cents—a dime apiece—are for:—
Gracie Roosevelt
Richard Derby II
Theodore Roosevelt III
Cornelius Van Schaak Roosevelt

Cornelius is the youngest. He is only about two months old. He is'n't as long as his name. But he will grow up to it. He is named after his great-great-grandfather, who when I was very small, over fifty years ago, helped teach me a Dutch baby-song. Little Richard is the eighth Richard Derby, from father to son, born here in America. He loves the bulldog—a nice, friendly, almost toothless bulldog. Little Ted is really Theodore IV; for my father was Theodore Roosevelt. He was the best man I ever knew; strong, fearless, gentle. *He* "feared God and took his own part"! Gracie is four. The other day her mother was giving her one of her first bible lessons.

Her mother said "Now, Gracie, remember that God made everything."
Gracie (much impressed) "Did He make *everything?*"
Her mother (with emphasis) "Yes; everything!"
Gracie (after a pause) "Well, He did'n't make my leggings fit very well; but I'm sure He meant to, so I wo'n't say anything about it!"

The other sixty cents are for my other six grandchildren. They are not born yet. If they are girls I think some of them will be named Edith, Alice, Ethel, Eleanor and Belle. If they are boys some of them will be named Kermit, Archie, Quentin and Jonathan Edwards. Jonathan Edwards was an ancestor of their grandmother's who lived in Colonial times. He was a great preacher and a strong and good man. I do'n't agree with all his theology; but his life teaches the two lessons which are more important than all others for the Americans of today; for he always acted in accordance with the strongest sense of duty, and there was'n't a touch of the mollycoddle about him. *Your friend*

Theodore Roosevelt

WILLIAM H. TAFT (1909–1913)

Two of William Howard Taft's three children, Robert (b. 1889) and Helen (b. 1891), reached their majority during their father's single term of office. The youngest, Charles (b. 1897), was, during the presidential years, a pupil in his uncle Horace's Taft School in Watertown, Connecticut. Since all three children were usually in school, or traveling, and away from home (especially when home was the White House), many of Taft's letters to young people are to his own children, often amusing, sometimes admonishing. Perhaps both traits emerge in a letter to Helen in which he observes, "I think your spelling in one or two instances was original, that is different from the way most of us spell, but I was able to understand what you meant, even if you did not follow Mr Noah Webster in his dictionary."

Taft could be equally wry in letters to other young people, even while following the rules so rigidly that he denied a girl's plea that her cadet brother at West Point, under discipline for an infraction, be given a waiver so that he could attend her wedding. Such Taft letters, although few, were rarely stuffy and official-sounding, even if outrageous. No underling appeared to be grinding out responses for him to append a signature. The letters, however, diminish in number through his four years in office, as if his burdens left him less and less time for smaller cares. Ira T. Smith, his White House mailroom clerk, recalled that Taft "didn't read letters if he could avoid it, and only the most important ones ever reached him. Even these were briefed so that he could get through them quickly." What Taft usually saw of his less-urgent mail was a list of letter writers, hometowns, and a summary of contents prepared for him. If he was interested in any of them, he would call for the originals. He seldom did.

A one-term president because his former crony and sponsor, Theodore Roosevelt, had not enjoyed his four years out of office and put himself forward in a third-party candidacy that split the Republican vote, Taft went on to other satisfying things. Disliking politics in any case, he took a professorship at the Yale Law School and then was named to the Supreme Court as chief justice. In his additional careers, he accumulated a mountain of additional correspondence. His letters here are limited to the presidency.

William Howard Taft to Robert Taft
Robert, at school, learns that his mother's stroke isn't nearly as important as a presidential ceremonial engagement.

The White House
May 18, 1909

My dear Robert:
You doubtless saw in this morning's papers that your mother had a nervous attack yesterday, and I write to you to tell what it is. You know she has had these attacks which seem to proceed from nervous exhaustion, and in which her heart functions very feebly. It is not an organic trouble of the

heart, but it seems to be some nervous affection. Yesterday she went to the hospital to be in attendance while Charley was having his throat cleaned of adenoids and tonsils, and I am afraid she was pretty well excited and tired over being there during the operation, thought she did not see it. She then came back with me to the White House, and we went down to the navy yard to get aboard the Sylph on our way to Mount Vernon. We had hardly pulled out in the stream when George Wickersham, who had been talking to your mother, said something which she did not answer. He said it again and she failed to answer, and then he noticed that she looked as if she had fainted. She did not lose consciousness, but she did have a very severe nervous attack, in which for the time being she lost all muscular control of her right arm and her right leg, and of her vocal chords and the muscles governing her speech. We came back as soon as her condition was fully ascertained, and brought her to the White House, where Dr. DeLaney was waiting, and he gave her some stimulant for her heart, which was very weak, and she was put to bed. She soon recovered control of her leg and arm, but she has not yet been able to speak. Of course these symptoms were very alarming, because they indicated paralysis—that is, a lesion in the brain. The doctor soon reassured us all, and her as well, because she could hear all right, that there was nothing of this kind—that it was a mere attack of nervous hysteria rather than a bursting of a bloodvessel in the brain, which is true paralysis. She slept well last night, had a good appetite, and slept well all day today. Charley, meantime, has come back from the hospital, and now has gone out to Charley Glover's, in the country, where he has retired for the night after having enjoyed himself hugely. Your mother is in good spirits now, although she can not talk. It breaks up a visit which she had planned to make with me to Petersburg and to Charlotte, but it will give her three or four days of rest, which she sorely needs.

I shall go tonight to Petersburg for tomorrow, and to Charlotte, North Carolina, for the next day. It will be a pretty hard and tiresome trip, but I have promised to go, and although I should like to stay with your mother, her condition is not such as to require it, and when such preparations are made as have been made for the reception of the President, he has no right to break his engagement except for some imperative reason.

As ever,

Your loving father,
Wm. H. Taft

William Howard Taft to Master Gordon H. Stoy

San Antonio, Texas
October 18, 1909

My dear Boy:

I have your letter in which you say you are President of the Rossville Boys Diamond Jubilee Club, and that you have bought some land near your father's. I am very glad to know that you are going into the farming business and expect to carry it on so efficiently.

With best wishes and thanks for your welcome, I am,
Sincerely yours,
Wm. H. Taft

William Howard Taft to Helen Taft

Vicksburg, Miss.,
October 28, 1909

My dear Helen:

Your mother sent me a letter the other day which you had written her, in which you complained that you were given stunts in English composition that you did not feel yourself quite equal to. I hope you will be as careful as possible in your writing and in the accuracy of your spelling and in the formation of your sentences. Your tendency like mine is to be sloppy, and we must restrict that tendency as far as we can.

I have gotten now down on the Mississippi and have traveled now about 12,000 miles out of 13,000. I am in excellent condition except that I have gained a number of pounds in flesh and my voice has been in a bad condition but is getting better. I have seen millions of people, have been most cordially received, and am very much pleased with the relations established between the Executive and the people I have seen. I am looking forward with great pleasure to seeing your mother again on the 10th of November, if I carry out the itinerary. Carpenter writes that your mother's condition is greatly improved and that her fluency of speech is very much more marked than it was at Beverly. She seems willing now to see people and anxious to try herself in a restricted social way.

I don't know what you are studying, my dear girl, but I hope that you will put in good licks on German and French, because I should like to have you an accomplished linguist.

I look forward with a great deal of pleasure to seeing you during the Christmas holidays, and possibly of getting a glimpse of you during Thanksgiving. I have one or two more trips to make immediately after my return, but they will be short ones and I shall then settle down to a steady life in the White House. I send you a great deal of love and best wishes for your current year.

Your loving father,
W.H.T.

William Howard Taft to Charles Taft, 2nd
Charley was at his uncle Horace's preparatory school in Watertown, Connecticut.

Vicksburg, Miss.,
October 28, 1909

My dear Charley:

I have seen one letter written by you to your mother, and I fear you have been rather lax in keeping up your communications with her. I presume that your time is largely taken up with lessons and with football, or out door sports, so that the writing of letters is rather a burden. But I hope you will cultivate it sufficiently to make it an easy thing for you in the future. Letters are of great advantage especially when one is traveling or engaged in work of interest, historical or otherwise. They serve the purpose of a diary and give in a succinct narrative form an account at the time of the things which have happened.

I saw a letter from you to your mother in which you said that the Blues had been beaten by the Browns. I inferred that you were among the Blues, and that therefore you were still bluer by reason of the result. But that fate is not the worst one that can happen. I suppose you would feel like going down to New Haven to see the game between Princeton and Harvard.

I am going to run up into Connecticut on Saturday after I return, but I shall be back in Washington on Sunday morning. I fear therefore I shall not be able to see you.

I am very sorry to hear of your Aunt Winifred's condition and hope that the treatment which she is to receive will bring about a complete recovery. I fear your poor Uncle Horace is greatly burdened by the illness of your Aunt and the carrying on of the school as well. I sincerely hope that he will not break down.

I have now been traveling within about 1500 miles of the full trip. I send you an itinerary so that you can follow it on the map if you choose. We are now between Memphis and Vicksburg and do not expect to reach Vicksburg until eight tonight. That relieves me from making speeches every hour of the day, and I take it as a great rest. Tomorrow we visit Natchez and possibly some other Louisiana towns, but on the next morning we reach New Orleans, where I shall probably have a great time because that city is a very hospitable one.

Good bye, my dear boy, I am glad to hear you are getting along well with your lessons and that your standard is higher than it was last year.

Your loving father,
W.H.T.

P.S. It is a great pleasure to hear from Mr. Carpenter that your mother is improving rapidly in the matter of speaking, that she is much more fluent now than she was at Beverly. The tone of her letters indicates too that she is in a happy frame of mind which means a great deal in the struggle she is making for complete recovery.

William Howard Taft to Charles Taft, 2nd

January 31, 1910

Charles P. Taft, second,
Care Horace D. Taft,
Watertown, Connecticut.

You have not written your mother since you left Washington. What is the matter with you?

WM. H. TAFT.

(private account)*

WOODROW WILSON (1913–1921)

From the White House, Woodrow Wilson wrote hundreds of letters to children. Having been an educator (his final post was as president of Princeton University, after which he became governor of New Jersey and then president of the United States), he had a natural tendency to break through the wall of

---

*This meant that the president paid for his personal postage.

Executive Office functionaries, an increasing breed, to write directly to children. Many letters were responses to courtesies offered, from flowers—and even a bird—presented to him by schoolchildren, to condolences offered on the death of his first wife. But some answered children seeking jobs for their fathers, communicated with young (and poor) relatives he was helping educate, and exhorted young people seeking advice or furnished a public message to a youth group. Even the association of newspaper delivery boys in Baltimore received a message, delivered as always in his austere, executive manner. Now and then the sheer surprise of a letter's contents would cause him to break out of bureaucratic—or ministerial—responses. Other exceptions to his official prose were his letters to his grandchildren, these written (or dictated) in his post-presidential invalidism, at the close of a life restricted by a stroke in his last year of office.

As World War I, which began during Wilson's first term, drew the nation closer and closer to open involvement, the life of the chief executive became too harried to answer as much personal mail as before. Yet his letters to children never ceased. He had a strong sense of the image of his office. Since that required that young people view the presidency positively, Wilson would put aside other business briefly to write to his young friends.

Woodrow Wilson to the Children of the Trenton (N.J.) Schools

The White House
April 4, 1913

My dear young Friends:

In sending you this greeting I naturally think of what you may make of yourselves, and of the great good you may do the country by making something of yourselves that is noble and worth while.

I have had a great deal to do with teaching young people, and it has sometimes discouraged and saddened me to feel that they thought that the school work was a bore and that the only real thing was the thing they were set free to do after school hours. I have had as much fun as anybody in my time and hope that you will have unlimited good times, but I wish I could make you realize now that play has nothing in it unless back of it lies good honest hard work, fitted to harden the fibre of every part of the mind and make it an instrument that we can work with, achieve with, conquer with, and do what we please with. The really happy men and women are the men and women who can do their job, and the men and women who can do their job best are those who have given themselves the best discipline and training. If you make the most of yourselves, you will be able to give a great gift of duty finely performed to the country which we all love and which we all ought to try to serve by making our own lives what we should like to have everybody believe the life of every American to be. My exhortation is, be sample Americans and make the sample very fine.

Faithfully yours,
Woodrow Wilson

Woodrow Wilson to Miss Ellen W. Erwin, Charlotte, North Carolina

[The White House, Washington, D.C.]
May 20, 1913

My dear Miss Ellie:

Mrs. Wilson has handed me your letter to her of the sixteenth. I wish I could hold out some prospect that I might find an appointment for your father, but I am sorry to say that it is not possible for me to do so, because I have made it a principle to regard the offices at my disposal as belonging to the public and not to myself, and, therefore, I have not felt at liberty to bestow them upon my personal friends. I wish that it were otherwise, but I think a little thought will convince you that it was my duty to take this position with regard to them.

We are very sorry that there is some possibility of your father's losing his present position and I sincerely wish him the best fortune.

In haste,

Cordially and sincerely yours,
Woodrow Wilson

Woodrow Wilson to the Children of the Methodist Orphanage in Raleigh, North Carolina

[The White House, Washington, D.C.]
December 23, 1913

My dear Little Friends:

I wish with all my heart that I could send you your good friend Secretary [of the Navy] Daniels to be with you on Christmas Day, but, unhappily, he is obliged in conscience to be here on that day. He will, however, be free to come after Christmas and expects, I believe, to be in Raleigh on Saturday. I cannot help hoping that this arrangement instead of depriving you of your usual Christmas pleasures will really give you two Christmases, Thursday and Saturday. We have learned to have as warm an affection for Secretary Daniels as evidently you have and I am going to take the liberty of sending you all my love through him.

With wishes for a very merry double Christmas,

Faithfully yours,
Woodrow Wilson

Woodrow Wilson to Miss Martha Berry, Berry School, Mt. Berry, Georgia

The White House
November 21, 1914

My dear Miss Berry:

Thank you sincerely for your kindness in sending me the pictures of the young ladies who carried the beautiful flowers to Mrs. Wilson's grave. Will you not let me express at the same time my very deep interest in the school and in all that concerns it? Mrs. Wilson had its welfare very much at heart and, therefore, it touches me very deeply that the children of the school should think of her as of a true friend who is gone.

I am glad to find the fame of the school spreading rapidly in this part of the country and hope that as it is better known it will be more and more generously supported.

Cordially and sincerely yours,
Woodrow Wilson

Woodrow Wilson to the Pupils of the Primary School at Rue de Fetinne, Liege, Belgium

The White House
April 2, 1915

My dear young Friends:

Your letter of February sixteenth, which the American Consul at Liege has sent me, has given me a great deal of pleasure. Americans have felt it to be a privilege to do what they could to help in relieving the distress in Belgium and they are sufficiently rewarded by such friendship and gratitude as your beautiful letter expresses.

Sincerely your friend,
Woodrow Wilson

Woodrow Wilson to the Newsboys of Baltimore

The White House
April 7, 1915

My dear Boys:

I am very glad to hear about the way in which you youngsters are beginning to take care of yourselves and stop the things that you are sure to be sorry for afterwards, and I want to send you this message of hearty good will and express the hope that the things you are learning now will make you not only more successful men, but happier men. The right road is the straight road and it is the only road that will carry any man where he would care to go, because I am sure that you feel as I do, that it isn't worth while to go anywhere if you cannot go with honor and self-respect. My message is God bless you and guide you!

Sincerely yours,
Woodrow Wilson

WARREN G. HARDING (1921–1923)

No president ever looked more like the idealized image of one than the white-maned, immaculately tailored Warren Gamaliel Harding. A compromise candidate in 1920, when Republican convention delegates could not agree upon one of their authentic leaders, Harding ran with the confidence that the presidency was largely a ceremonial position from which he could delegate the real work. Although his administration included substantial figures like Herbert Hoover, Andrew Mellon, and Charles Evans Hughes, they are overshadowed in history by Harding's sleazy cronies. A few of them, including two Cabinet members, were convicted of misusing their offices. Particularly remembered is the Teapot Dome oil-lease scandal. But by then, Harding was dead. Ignoring serious medical symptoms, he had succumbed on a railway trip to the West. He had feared, but did not live to see, the disgrace of his friends and the damage to his own reputation.

The public in Harding's lifetime had not known how tawdry was the man behind the presidential facade. Harding had married a wealthy and much older woman, Florence Kling, who attempted to manage his political ascent. The marriage was childless, but Harding may not have been. Among his indiscreet affairs appears to have been one with an emotional Ohio girl with a frizzy topknot, Nan Britton, whom he had met when she was fourteen. After his death, she published a scandalous memoir, *The President's Daughter*. If Harding had kept up a fervid secret correspondence with her, as Nan claimed, the letters have not survived other than in her descriptions of them. Her child did, but Harding's parentage was never proved, and only the intense secretiveness of Harding's family after his death, and continuing still through their resort to the courts, suggests that there may have been something to Nan's claims. Other affairs have been established and letters survive.

Some of Harding's meager presidential-period correspondence with young people appears genuine and sincere, although others suggest the hand of a stuffy aide. His secretary, George Christian, usually responded to juvenile mail with a form letter advising "that the President is confronted by an extraordinary burden of public and personal duties," but he was not able to intercept everything. Harding sometimes answered mail that should have been replied to by a low-level assistant, as he enjoyed working late at night (when he was not playing poker and drinking with his friends), answering crackpot letters and the occasional letters from children. According to Francis Russell's biography, *The Secret of Blooming Grove* (1968):

> He promised to buy tickets from an eleven-year-old boy raising funds for a swimming pool, and recalled the Caledonia Creek he used to swim in. To the maker of Dodson's Bird Houses and Famous Sparrow Trap, who wished to convert the White House grounds to a bird sanctuary, he replied with thanks, asking the inventor to postpone his project "for the present." He declined a silver Persian kitten born on [his] Inauguration Day. A female schoolteacher begged him . . . as his body was "the Temple of the Holy Ghost" to quit the use of tobacco and "let me know when you quit." He complimented her sincerity but did not "look upon the habit with quite so much horror as you do and think you attach over-much importance to my moderate use of it." Harding's files became clogged with such correspondence and his hundreds of replies.

Once Nicholas Murray Butler, president of Columbia University (to whose daughter Teddy Roosevelt had written), found Harding in his White

House office staring at a pile of letters that he groaned about not having time to answer. Butler asked if he could look at some and found that they were too trivial for a president to bother with. "I suppose so," Harding agreed, "but I am not fit for this office and should never have been here."

The letter about Harding's boyhood swimming hole has not been located in his White House papers. A few others to children survive. One to a boy in Florida demonstrates that Harding's reading tastes, as well as his spelling, were execrable. Other letters reveal a man who lacked imagination but not sympathy. As he confessed to Butler, the office overwhelmed him.

Warren G. Harding to Miss Alice E. Strock
The daughter of the minister at the First Presbyterian Church in Harding's hometown of Marion, Ohio, sought a Columbia scholarship. Nicholas Murray Butler, a pillar of the Republican Party, was university president. Harding's intervention worked.

Washington, D.C.
March 2, 1922

My dear Miss Strock:
I have your letter of February eighteenth. Since its receipt I have had a personal interview with Dr. Butler of Columbia and, though the application comes exceedingly late for favorable action this year, he has promised me that he will give it his personal attention and undertake to put the fellowship through for you. At his suggestion, I have sent him your letter and that of Miss Windate. I hope you will hear from it favorably in a very short time.

It is a pleasure to be of this little service.

With very best wishes, I am

Sincerely yours,
Warren G. Harding

Warren G. Harding to Phoebe Randolph Harding

Washington, D.C.
July 8, 1922

My dear Miss Harding:
On returning from Ohio I find your pleasing letter. It is not possible for me to sit down and scratch you a line in my rather illegible hand writing,

but I am happy to make an acknowledgment of your letter and assure you that I am pleased to know there is a Phoebe Randolph Harding in North Carolina. I am very partial to the name of Phoebe, probably because that was my dear mother's name, and she was a very good and noble woman. She had an older sister by the name of Abbie and my next youngest sister is named Abigail in her honor. So you see the names you mention are quite familiar to me, and I am exceedingly fond of them.

I am grateful to you for your very kindly wishes, and can have no argument with you about your political affiliations. I think nearly everybody must be Democratic in party affiliation in your great state. After all it does not so much matter what our party preferences are if we are devoted to country before party.

Permit me to express to you my very cordial compliments and good wishes.

Very truly yours,
Warren G. Harding

Warren G. Harding to Miss Dolly Acklin
Since a number of children did write to Harding about their mutual birthdate, it is curious that Harding responded, rather, to a girl born on a different date. One must suspect, given the Nan Britton affair, that Harding was attracted—harmlessly, this time—by the photograph that the girl from Oil City, Pennsylvania, included.

Washington, D.C.
November 4, 1922

Dear Dolly:

Thank you for the copy of your picture which you sent to me. I see that you were born on November eleventh, which comes pretty close to being my birthday. A great many of my little friends who were born on November second, as I was, have written to me. After seeing your picture, I cannot help wishing you might have joined the company and picked our birthday for your own purpose. I hope you may have a great many happy anniversaries of the day.

Sincerely your friend,
Warren G. Harding

CALVIN COOLIDGE (1923–1929)

Harding's successor found ways to keep the office from overwhelming him. A reluctant president, he was also a reluctant correspondent. When, by the light of a kerosene lamp in his farmhouse at Plymouth Notch, Vermont, Vice President John Calvin Coolidge took the oath of office on August 2, 1923, replacing the dead Harding, nothing in Coolidge's dour personality or philosophy of limited government changed. He said little, wrote little, and did little as president, yet the formula seemed to work. Times were good and proceeded to get better.

The volume of letters to the president increased, many urging him to run for election in his own right in 1924. Children wrote to him too, asking for help on class projects, for statements of principle for their school newspapers, for the opening of a boys' club, or for the beginning of Girls' Week. Some well-wishers (or the merely curious) even wrote to his two sons, and he demanded to see all such correspondence they received. Most writers to the president received replies from an assistant regretting "that the President has been compelled to make his excuses to friends presenting this kind of request to him. As you may imagine, the number of such requests that come to him is astonishingly large; indeed, if he were to deal with all of them, they would greatly impose upon his time and energies which must be protected for his public duties."

When Coolidge agreed to run in 1924, he carried on the most inactive campaign of the century. His younger son, Calvin, Jr., had died on July 7, 1924, of septicemia following a foot blister that had seemed trivial. Coolidge had then withdrawn still further and became even more protective of his surviving son, John, upon whom he lavished all of his New England Yankee scrutiny. During the campaign—which Coolidge waged by waving now and then from a train or from his front porch—young John began his freshman year at Amherst College, in Northampton, Massachusetts. "I can remember feeling, especially when I was an undergraduate," John wrote two generations later, "that my father as a correspondent was at times rather too accomplished in the succinct, forthright, and comprehensive communication of his thoughts." Yet John Coolidge was rather lucky at that. Not only did he receive some of the very few letters by the president penned in his own hand from the White House, he also had a father who, despite the myriad of puritanical injunctions by which he harassed John in his undergraduate life, really cared.

Calvin Coolidge to His Son John Coolidge

> The White House
> Washington
> September 25, 1924.

My dear John:

You have not told us anything about what you are doing at Amherst, as to what you are studying, where you are boarding, how many members you have in your fraternity delegation, or anything of the kind. I want you to take a book and set down in it all your expenses, so that you will know for what you are paying out your money.

I am giving you a letter of introduction to Mr. Allis for you to give him. There will be things that you need to ask him about. He was in college with me in the Class of '93 I think. When you don't know what to do about anything, you can go and ask him. I have already indicated that I want you to stay in Amherst and study, and not be running to Northampton. If anybody invites you to go out evenings or anything of that kind, you will have to tell them that it is all you can do to take care of your work at the College. You are going to be there four years, and there will be time enough to do visiting after the first year.

> Yours father,
> Calvin Coolidge

We are sending you envelopes in which you will send here all letters from strangers.

Calvin Coolidge to His Son John Coolidge

> The White House
> Washington
> October 12 '24

My dear John:—

Some weeks ago I wrote you a letter. You have made no response to it whatever. When I send you some instructions I want to know that you are carrying them out.

Now I want to know how much time you are spending in Northampton. I would like to know what entertainments you are attending and who you are taking with you there and at Amherst.

I want you to keep in mind that you have been sent to college to work. Nothing else will do you any good. Nobody in my class who spent their time in other ways has ever amounted to anything. Unless you want to spend your time working you may just as well leave college. Nothing else will make you a man or gain for you the respect of people.

I want you to refuse all requests that will interfere with your doing the work that is assigned each day for you to do.

Your father,
Calvin Coolidge

Calvin Coolidge to His Son John Coolidge

The White House
Washington
Aug. 5, 1925

My dear John:—

You are going to decide about now whether you will amount to anything. Whether you will be a creature with all the weaknesses of a woman with some of her graces or whether you will really grow up to be a man. You will make this decision for the most part by determining whether you will work or loaf. You can't change yourself in a day, you may think working does no good but in a short time it will tell. You will have to decide now. A year from now will be too late. The world will pass on and leave you and you will see many boys that you do not think are very smart going right by you and leaving you behind to be ignored, pitied and despised.

You will have to make this decision yourself. No one can make it for you. But unless you work I do not propose to pay out money to let you idle around college.

Your father
Calvin Coolidge

Calvin Coolidge to His Son John Coolidge

The White House
Washington
October 13, 1925

My dear John:

I have your request for another check which is enclosed. I noticed that in your last statement before this one you had what I should judge was a pressing ticket, $5.00, but in this one you have $1.50 for getting your clothes pressed. I wish you would explain those two items to me. You do not need to spend very much money getting your clothes pressed. If it is done once in three weeks or so, it is often enough. Your every-day clothes do not need pressing more often than that and your better clothes will pretty much straighten out when they are hung in the closet. I should like to know how you are getting on in your studies. I wish you would send me the name of each Professor that you are under and the subject that he is teaching you. You have a very easy course this year as you had French before, and in French you ought to be very close to perfect.

Your father,
Calvin Coolidge

HERBERT HOOVER (1929–1933)

On becoming president after serving in the Cabinets of Harding and Coolidge, Herbert Clark Hoover, a millionaire engineer, brought a level of management to the White House that eliminated the comparative simplicity of style he had inherited. Instead, he established a multilevel staff of political, press, and administrative assistants that insulated him from such minor distractions as children. Still, some mail was permitted through, perhaps in a public-relations move to humanize the office after Coolidge, and Hoover wrote, for example, to the second-grade class of the Bywood School in Upper Darby, Pennsylvania, that its letter (in neat, one-inch-high penmanship) "gave me a moment of warmest pleasure in a busy day and I thank you for it." In other letters, he politely turned down an invitation to an eighth-grade graduation in Clifton Hill, Missouri; sent a note for insertion in a Grand Haven, Michigan, girl's autograph book; offered the White House pet opossum as mascot to the Hyattsville, Maryland, high school athletic teams; and—ever the engineer—complimented a Painesville, Ohio, boy on his efficient dam building. And he pressed his conservative, do-it-yourself, small-government philosophy upon a Columbus, Ohio, girl who wanted to send "old blankets and clothes, shoes and food" to the White House for distribution to the poor.

Although during Hoover's single-term presidency, the chief executive responded directly to few letters from young people, most of those that Hoover did answer personally (unlike that to the girl seeking federal coordination of aid to the poor) demonstrate a warmth that many of his political critics thought was absent from his personality. During his post-presidential years, when his time was more free, he replied often to children who continued to write to him as that rare American phenomenon, an ex-president. (Two had already died in office since 1900.) In 1962, Hoover published a small volume of his mail to and from children, *On Growing Up, Letters to American Boys and Girls*. It omitted, "in fairness to the youngsters," wrote Hoover in his preface, the names and addresses of his correspondents. Those letters reproduced here from his post-presidential years are thus without surnames.

Herbert Hoover to Robert M. Venemann

Hyattsville High School, in Maryland, acquired the White House opossum, Billy, as mascot in the spring of 1929 and proceeded to win the Prince Georges County high school championships in soccer, basketball, track, and baseball. The students, returning Billy, thanked the president for the measure of good luck "Billy Possum" had brought to their athletic program.

> *The White House*
> *Washington*
> *July 13, 1929*

My dear Robert:

I am glad to have your formal report on the efficiency of Billy Opossum—it will be incorporated into his service record. Precautions will be taken to maintain his health and spirits for the further needs of the Prince Georges County High School teams.

> *Yours faithfully,*
> *Herbert Hoover*

Herbert Hoover to Milton H. Campbell

Reading that Hoover had been building a dam on a stream at his summer home in Virginia, and that the president's guests had been assisting with the construction, thirteen-year-old Milton Campbell reported to the president that he had been doing the same thing in Painesville, Ohio, and enlisted his friends in the project. With the letter came engineering details of the forty-foot dam, which made both swimming and stocking possible above it, and two photographs.

> *The White House*
> *Washington*
> *September 14, 1929*

My dear Milton:

I have received your very kind note of September 8th with its enclosures. It is certainly a fine dam you have constructed, I believe better than those on which I have been engaged lately. I am glad to note that you like to work out of doors. It is good for us all.

> Yours faithfully,
> Herbert Hoover

Herbert Hoover to Barbara Jane McIntyre
Ten-year-old Barbara McIntyre and her friends, concerned over the distress of the poor during the Depression winter of 1931, just beginning, wrote to the president from Columbus, Ohio, that they were planning to collect old blankets, clothing, and shoes, as well as food, to send him in Washington for distribution to the needy. Also, she wrote, they were going to take up a weekly collection, no contribution to be more than a dime, for the same purpose. Hoover's response was in keeping with his conservative philosophy.

> The White House
> Washington
> November 19, 1931

My dear Barbara:

I have your very sweet letter of November 10th. It is a very beautiful undertaking. I would suggest, however, that instead of sending the contributions which you collect to me, that you should yourself distribute them to those who are in need in your own locality.

> Yours faithfully,
> Herbert Hoover

Herbert Hoover to Martin ———

Dear Mr. Hoover,

I am a boy 10 years old and who would like to become President like you when I grow up. I thought that if I wrote to you that you can give me some information how you got to be a President. I wish you would send me an autograph. I would like that very much.

> Your friend,
> Martin ———

Dear Martin:

I am in favor of your ambition to be President. As to your request on the rules as to "how to get to be President," I suggest that:

The first rule is just to be a boy getting all the constructive joy out of life.

The second rule is that no one should win the Presidency without honesty and sportsmanship and consideration for others in his character—together with religious faith.

The third rule is that he should be a man of education.

If you follow these rules, you will be a man of standing in your community even if you do not make the White House. And who can tell? Maybe that also.

Yours faithfully,
Herbert Hoover

Herbert Hoover to Stephen ———

Stephen was a son of a friend of Hoover's who had lunched with Hoover and his father at the White House, but no one among his schoolmates would believe him. The button Hoover refers to was a George Washington Bicentennial commemorative of 1932.

February 2, 1933

My dear Stephen:

This is to certify that you lunched at the White House with me. I have never been strong on spinach myself, and I had meant to tell you that you didn't have to eat it.

In order to make sure that you remember that you were at the White House, I am sending you herewith a button which you are entitled to wear as proof thereof.

Yours faithfully,
Herbert Hoover

Herbert Hoover to Kathy ———

Dear President Hoover:

My Dad thinks you are the smartest living president, so I would like to have your opinion on this question: What are the chances of there ever being a woman president of the United States?

Best wishes to you,

Sincerely,
Kathy ———

[no date, but post-1933]

My dear Kathy:

As a generalization, the men have not done too good a job of government in the world in the last forty-seven years, and the chances for the women are thereby increased.

With good wishes to you if you are a candidate for President about thirty years hence.

*Yours faithfully,
Herbert Hoover*

Herbert Hoover to Shirley ———
Shirley had written to the aged ex-president that her class "is writing the important men of the United States to find out what Christmas means to them." His crusty response was devoid of Yuletide sentimentality.

[no date, but ca. 1950–1960]

Dear Shirley:

What does Christmas mean to me?

1. We have gone through another year without war.

2. We still have enough left after taxes to buy a Christmas tree and trim it properly.

3. Some of my children, grandchildren, and great-grandchildren will come to see me and the tree.

4. There will be too much to eat.

5. And I wish for all of you in your class a Merry Christmas and a Good New Year.

*Yours faithfully,
Herbert Hoover*

FRANKLIN DELANO ROOSEVELT (1933–1945)

Although Franklin Delano Roosevelt served longer than any other president and received—and wrote—many thousands of letters while in the White House, very few of his younger correspondents ever received a letter he prepared himself. There were just too many. Disabled by poliomyelitis more than he would ever admit until the last year of his life, and beset by the demands of economic depression and world war, he had, despite his warm public manner, little time or energy for personal letters. Even polio victims writing to him about his favorite charitable cause, the March of Dimes, or about their own battles with paralysis, rarely received a letter he drafted or dictated himself. Most of his letters were not only written by, but signed by, Louis McHenry Howe, Stephen Early, William Hassett, Missy Le Hand, and Grace Tully. Few letters reveal his own special quality of wit or the compassion he deeply felt and that inspired his public statements, speeches, and the course of his policies.

One of the rare letters seemingly entirely his own was written not to a young constituent, but to a young dachshund, Noodle, to thank Noodle for the package of Christmas cookies he had sent to FDR's Scottie, Fala. The pet of his friend, the popular historian Hendrik Willem Van Loon, Noodle Van Loon added a note envying the railway rides a presidential dog received. To Noodle, Fala replied on December 23, 1940, with Roosevelt's assistance that "the long rides on swaying cars over rolling wheels—just like five thousand mile cruises to see a lot of islands—ain't no fun for us folk. . . . I prefer to walk in the yards where trees grow and there is some place to scratch." We see there the wit of the famous Teamsters Union speech of the 1944 campaign, in which Roosevelt castigated Republicans not so much for personal attacks on him and his family, but for their slanders of Fala. The defense of Fala became one of the memorable quips of the election year.

FDR's mail at the White House was enormous throughout his presidency. During his first seven days as president, in March 1933, he received 450,000 letters and telegrams. His letter-writing staff was too overwhelmed to even attempt to capture the easy, relaxed style associated with the man, although every reply, according to White House instructions, was at least to contain an allusion to something specific the writer had said, to demonstrate that the letter had indeed been read. (Some later presidents were not that careful.) Of the thousands of letters to young polio victims or to juvenile contributors to the March of Dimes, perhaps a few hundred over the years were signed by the president, and most of these were form responses with minor variations. An eager consumer of data that might reflect public opinion, he was interested in analyses of his mail, but children did not vote and often wrote to Roosevelt because they shared his physical affliction—or his hobby.

The president's correspondence about stamp collecting ran into the thousands of letters, many writers contributing stamps, but only a few schoolchildren (usually with politically connected parents) received stamps from him or a letter signed by FDR himself. Letters about birthdays and accolades for youthful courage were other large groups of responses, but few were actually signed by the president. Requests for substantive things, whether begging letters or not, had to be deflected or ignored—leaving one to wonder how the course of history might have been changed if young Fidel Castro had received his wish. Queries about his life, habits, and opinions from schoolchildren seeking an autograph through that subterfuge or material for a class assignment were usually responded to by such a letter as Steve Early's: "So many requests similar to yours come to him that he has no alternative except to decline to answer any of them. I think on reflection you will understand why it is necessary for him to pursue this course. He never varies from his rule to confine consideration of public questions to his public addresses and to his conferences with the press." Thus one facet of his personality rarely emerged through his letters to his youngest correspondents. Perhaps Fala should have written more of them.

Franklin D. Roosevelt to Le Roy Johnson

A neighbor of Le Roy Johnson, a boy stricken with infantile paralysis, wrote not to FDR, but to Mrs. Eleanor Roosevelt, whose compassion as first lady was already well realized around the country before the president's first year of office had run its course. In her letter, the neighbor, Mrs. Emma Zander, noted that the boy, sixteen, the son of a streetcar motorman, had been both an athlete and a violinist before his illness, had not shown any improvement, and was becoming discouraged. What Mrs. Zander appealed for was a cheering letter from Mrs. Roosevelt, but she sent the letter instead to her husband's secretary Missy Le Hand for a higher-level response.

The White House
February 7, 1934.

My dear Le Roy:

I have just learned that you were stricken with infantile paralysis last fall. I am awfully sorry and I want to write you personally to give you if I can a word of cheer. Do exactly what the doctors tell you and keep up the same fine courage you put into your athletics—put all you have got into the determination to get better and you will win out.

My very best wishes go to you with this note.

Very sincerely yours,
Franklin D. Roosevelt

Franklin D. Roosevelt to Sherman Franklin, Jr.

*The White House
January 17, 1934.*

My dear Sherman:

It has been a real pleasure to learn that we celebrate our birthdays on the same day.

I am writing not only to wish you the happiest possible birthday and many, many more; but also to tell you how much I hope you are making the most splendid progress toward recovery.

Keep up your courage!

*Very sincerely yours,
Franklin D. Roosevelt*

Franklin D. Roosevelt to Robert Kennedy
Robert Kennedy, younger brother of the future president and later attorney general under John Kennedy, had an influential father who was, during FDR's first two terms, a power in the Democratic Party, chairman of the Securities and Exchange Commission, and later ambassador to Great Britain. Roosevelt wrote to young Bobby Kennedy at Hyannisport, Massachusetts.

July 12, 1935.

Dear Bob:—

Your Dad has told me that you are a stamp collector and I thought you might like to have these stamps to add to your collection. I am also enclosing a little album which you may find useful.

Perhaps sometime when you are in Washington you will come in and let me show you my collection.

My best wishes to you.

*Very sincerely yours,
Franklin D. Roosevelt*

*Hyannisport, Massachusetts
July 19, 1935*

Dear Mr. President,

I liked the stamps you sent me very much, and the little book is very useful. I am just starting my collection and it would be great fun to see yours which mother says you have had for a long time.

I am going to frame your letter and I am going to keep it always in my room.

Daddy, Mother and all my brothers and sisters want to be remembered to you.

Bobby Kennedy

Franklin D. Roosevelt to Miss Shirley Temple

Shirley Temple was nine and America's most famous moppet when she helped celebrate FDR's fifty-sixth birthday in 1938. As an adult, she shifted allegiance to the other party, in whose ranks she prospered.

The White House
February 15, 1938

Dear Shirley:

That wonderful birthday cake made us all happy on January thirtieth, and my only complaint is that I ate too much of it.

When you come to Washington I do hope you will come in to see me.

As ever your friend,
Franklin D. Roosevelt

Fidel Castro to Franklin Delano Roosevelt

The future revolutionary leader of Cuba, a schoolboy when FDR was elected to his third term in 1940, already evidenced, although in inadequate English, a youthful arrogance and ambition unusual in a twelve-year-old. Although his appeal was preserved in the White House files, no letter in return has been located. The Colegio de Delores was a Jesuit school that Castro attended until 1942.

Colegio de Dolores
Santiago de Cuba
Nov. 6, 1940

Mr. Franklin Roosevelt
President of the United States

My good friend Roosevelt

I don't know very English, but I know as much as write to you.

I like to hear the radio, and I am very happy, because I heard in it that you will be President for a new (periodo).

I am twelve years old. I am a boy but I think very much but I do not think that I am writting to the President of the United States.

If you like, give me a ten dollars bill green american, in the letter because never I have not seen a ten dollars bill green american and I would like to have one of them. My address is

  Sr. Fidel Castro
  Colegio de Dolores
  Santiago de Cuba
  Oriente, Cuba

I don't know very English but I know very much Spanish and I suppose you don't know very Spanish but you know very English because you are American but I am not American.

(Thank you very much) Good by. Your friend,
Fidel Castro

If you want iron to make your ships I will show to you the bigest (minar) of iron of the land. They are in Mayari Oriente Cuba.

Franklin D. Roosevelt to Diana Hopkins

Diana Hopkins was the motherless daughter of FDR's aide and confidant Harry Hopkins. With the letter to Diana was enclosed a large FDR-drawn valentine.

February 5, 1941

Dear Diana:—

That was a very nice note you sent to me and I love my Valentine.

I miss you and hope that when Daddy gets home you will come down for a little visit.

Affectionately,
Franklin D. Roosevelt

Franklin D. Roosevelt to Peter II, King of Yugoslavia

Peter II of Yugoslavia was one of many child kings in Europe in the prewar years when kings still reigned even when they did not rule. When Hitler invaded Yugoslavia in 1941, young Peter became, also, one of the many kings in exile. In 1942, when he was still a teenager, FDR wrote to the secretary of state, "Will you try your hand at preparing a nice personal letter from me to the King of Yugoslavia? It can start off, 'Dear Peter', as I have always treated him as a sort of ward." The letter reproduced here is more stilted, signed by the president but in State Department rhetoric.

The White House
July 31, 1942

HIS MAJESTY
   PETER II,
      KING OF YUGOSLAVIA,
         LONDON.

Your Majesty's visit was a personal pleasure which I shall long remember. It gave also to the American people an opportunity to do honor to the valiant Yugoslav People in their noble and unceasing fight for the liberation of their country.

I noted with pleasure the energy and thoroughness with which you entered into the daily life of America at war, seeking out the men at work and studying the conversion of our great industries to the sole purpose of providing the armaments with which the war shall be won. I am glad that you carried with you the conviction of America's determination to press on to victory with everything we have.

Franklin D. Roosevelt

Franklin D. Roosevelt to Princess Margriet Francisca of the Netherlands (Telegram)

June 29, 1943

Love and congratulations and all good wishes to you on your christening day. Your Godfather wishes much that he could be there. Tell your Mother that she must bring you to Hyde Park very soon.

Franklin D. Roosevelt

HARRY S. TRUMAN (1945–1953)

Inundated by the responsibilities of his unanticipated presidency (Harry Truman did not know how ill FDR was in early 1945), Roosevelt's successor left the small talk of his office to his staff, at first inherited from his predecessor. As a result, after his letters to his teenage daughter from his days in the Senate, there are few letters to children that follow from his White House years. A little Missouri fifth-grader received a thank-you for a birthday greeting shortly after Truman became president, but very likely only because it was to be delivered by Truman's crony and military aide, Harry Vaughan. A thirteen-year-old who happened to be the niece of a presidential secretary received a letter, after his first plane ride, about Truman's own first flight, in France in 1918, when, "due to all the gyrations," he became airsick as a passenger in a "Jenny." A polio-stricken boy in a Dayton hospital who sent the president $1.49 after hearing a March of Dimes radio appeal received a rare personal letter, as did the son of Truman's physician, Howard Rusk, who was ill with pneumonia in St. Louis. The president invited him, once he was well again, to "come to the White House for a swim in my pool." Harry Truman's legendary feistiness is missing from his presidential correspondence with young people. His own letters show signs of haste, and his staff's responses are mostly kindly brush-offs, such as "To be fair to all, [he] has been forced to suspend the practice of autographing." His staff answered queries about his hobbies ("walking") and the names of books and authors he enjoyed as a boy (Mark Twain, the Henty boys books, the Bible, and *Silas Marner*). When children sent pennies to augment Truman's salary, the reply was "While your thought in sending the eleven cents is appreciated . . . , it is not possible to accept contributions."

Young writers sympathized with Truman's defense of his daughter's singing, despite *Washington Post* critic Paul Hume's undiplomatic aspersions. They also wondered what his mysterious middle name was. The response: "The 'S' in the President's name is an initial only. It seems that one of his grandfathers bore the name of Shippe and the other the name of Solomon; but he was not given either name."

Although the letters to children to which Truman put his name while president are few, during his nearly twenty years as ex-president he actually saw, and signed, most of the mail he generated as the nation's most visible exponent of the value of learning more history and of participating in government. It was not only the university professors researching his administration who wrote to him to ask about his motives and moves during the White House years—young people asked as well, and Truman, who was often brusque with the professors, answered many of the children's queries, sometimes furnishing footnotes to history not offered to the specialists. There, in the post-1952 letters, emerged the authentic Harry Truman.

Harry S. Truman to His Daughter Margaret

Truman was immensely busy during the early war years as chairman of a Senate committee overseeing the efficiency of the war production effort, and he was seldom home. His earlier letters to Bess Truman often had an aside to their daughter or a closing "Kiss Margie for me," but when Margaret turned seventeen, her father began writing letters to her—and expecting mail in return.

Springfield, Missouri
October 1, 1941

My dear Margie,

Your very nice letter came yesterday to the Melbourne Hotel in St. Louis. I am glad you like your Spanish and the teacher of it. In days to come it will be a most useful asset. Keep it up and when we get to the point when we can take our South American tour you can act as guide and interpreter.

Ancient History is one of the most interesting of all studies. By it you find out why a lot of things happen today. But you must study it on the basis of the biographies of the men and women who lived it. For instance, if you were listening in on the Senate committee hearings of your dad, you would understand why old Diogenes carried a lantern in the daytime in his search for an honest man. Most everybody is fundamentally honest, but when men or women are entrusted with public funds or trust estates of other people they find it most difficult to honestly administer them. I can't understand or find out why that is so—but it is.

You will also find out that people did the same things, made the same mistakes, and followed the same trends as we do today. For instance, the Hebrews had a republic three or four thousand years ago that was almost ideal in its practical workings. Yet they tired of it and went to a monarchy or totalitarian state. So did Greece, Carthage, Rome. . . . I'm glad you like Ancient History—wish I could study it again with you. Buy this month's National Geographic and see how like us ancient Egypt was. Here is a dollar to buy it with. You can buy soda pop with the change.

Lots of love to you,
Dad

Harry S. Truman to Susan Pauley

Susan Pauley began by informing Truman that her father, the president's friend and California political ally Ed Pauley, "does not know that I am writing this," and went on to describe her defense of his firing General MacArthur ("for the good of the country") to her schoolmates, most of whom came from wealthy, conservative households. MacArthur had just delivered his "old soldiers never die; they just fade away" speech to Congress. "I go," she wrote, "to a school called Marlborough, where the Democrats are definitely in the minority. We were allowed to listen to General MacArthur's speech during study period; and when everyone else was crying at the end of it, I couldn't help but think that it was very corny. Maybe this was because of what Daddy had already told me about General MacArthur when he knew him in Japan, and Mr. President, I really felt that *you* were right." Truman's mail had been running heavily against his sacking of the arrogant MacArthur, and before he had his secretary Rose Conway add the letter to the "Dismissal Pro" file, he wrote Susan an appreciative letter.

The White House
May 5, 1951

Dear Susan:

I can't tell you how very much I appreciated your lovely letter of April twenty-ninth. I am glad your mother was willing that you should send it to me. Mrs. Truman read it and thought it was a wonderful letter.

We receive so many letters that are not pleasant that when one such as yours is received it helps to make the day brighter.

I am glad you told your high school class what the facts are. I am enclosing three speeches which cover the situation completely and thoroughly and if you will read them you will know just about as much of the Foreign Policy of the United States as the President does.

Sincerely yours,
Harry S. Truman

Enclosures:
1. "Preventing a New World War" — April 11, 1951 — by the President.
2. "Our Far Eastern Policy"   — April 18, 1951 — by Sec/State.
3. Address at Jeff-Jackson Dinner — April 14, 1951 — by the President.

Harry S. Truman to Billy Taber
Billy Taber, an eighth-grade student in the Rowe School, Conneaut, Ohio, had written to ask what he should study in high school.

December 8, 1959

Dear Billy:

Replying to your letter of November 24 regarding a possible course of study to take in high school which would be beneficial to you, I will tell you what I think as a result of my long experience.

It would be well for you to take Latin because it is fundamental in the study of Italian, Spanish and French. There are thousands of words in the English language you can understand better if you know Latin.

A mathematical course including Algebra and Geometry is essential.

Both General History and a good History of the United States are most necessary.

In order to understand Composition and to learn how to read good literature intelligently you must study English and American Literature.

Also, you must have a basic knowledge of Physics before you finish your high school.

This looks like a great big load but if you arrange it right it will not work you too hard, especially if you are interested in these subjects; and it is good for a young man to improve his mind. I wish you luck in your studies, but remember, it takes plenty of hard work and anxiety to obtain knowledge.

Sincerely yours,
Harry S. Truman

Harry S. Truman to the Social Studies Class of Sequoia Junior High, Fontana, California

The class wrote to ex-president Truman that following the change of administration, from Eisenhower to Kennedy, "This may be the only time in history that there are four presidents living at the same time," and urged that a photograph be taken of the four. (The fourth would have been Hoover.) Truman found it an occasion for a history lesson.

Independence, Missouri
April 19, 1961

To the Sequoia Junior High School Students:

I more than appreciated yours of the 10th, and I am more than pleased at your interest in the present day living former Presidents and President of the United States.

For your information, in 1861 there were five former Presidents alive and when you count Mr. Lincoln, who was inaugurated in March of 1861, there were six. There was an effort made to get those five former Presidents and the new President together in the hope that a conference might stop the War Between the States, but it didn't work out.

I don't know whether it will ever be possible to obtain a picture of the President and the former Presidents or not. I hope that sometime it may be possible.

Sincerely yours,
Harry S. Truman

Harry S. Truman to David S. McCracken
McCracken, a Kentucky student, questioned why Truman didn't act as president to force Russia out of Hungary and other eastern European countries when postwar Soviet intentions to communize them became apparent. The John Birch Society, he implied, saw a Communist conspiracy at work in the United States to restrain American reaction.

Independence, Missouri
November 10, 1961

Dear Mr. McCracken:

In reply to the question in your letter of November 5th, at the time about which you write, the Russians had one hundred divisions on the Eastern Front and we had about a dozen.

There wasn't anything that could be done at the time. That was brought about by the fact that the people at home kept crying for their sons to be brought home and the sons kept crying, "I want to go home."

The John Birchers are just Ku Klux without the nightshirts and, of course, they don't know what the facts are.

Sincerely yours,
Harry S. Truman

Harry S. Truman to Val E. Osher
A party loyalist, Truman left no doubt as to where he stood. When eleven-year-old Susanne Coats wrote to him from Michigan in 1951 that her parents were Republicans but that she intended, when she grew up, to be a Democrat, then-president Truman complimented her on her decision, and the wire services, although misquoting her letter and Truman's response, made the exchange into news. The caption to a photo showing her reading the president's letter to her nine-month-old brother indicated that he had not yet decided on a party affiliation. As ex-president a decade later, Truman was his feisty self as he responded

bluntly to Val Osher's query from California about whether the only real difference in the two major political parties was their names.

Independence, Missouri
July 31, 1962

Dear Val:

In reply to your recent letter, the main difference between the Democratic and Republican Parties is that the Democratic Party is for helping the common everyday man and the Republican Party has the viewpoint that if you start at the top things will work out all right for those at the bottom and that is the reason I am a Democrat.

Sincerely yours,
Harry S. Truman

Harry S. Truman to Brendan T. Crowe
The trials of Nazi war criminals were held while Truman was president, and he defended the trials when a student at Syracuse University questioned them.

Independence, Missouri
August 30, 1962

Dear Brendan:

I read your letter of the 17th, with a great deal of interest. The objective of the Nurnberg Trials was to put on the record the reason for the punishment of the terrible war criminals who had slaughtered so many people so unmercifully.

There are those who think the trials and punishment of the war criminals were too severe but if they would go back and read their history they would find, of course, that these same criminals in times past would merely have been placed before the firing squad with no trials at all by the victors. I think the Trials were proper.

I am not going into any individual cases at this time but if you are ever in this area and would care to stop by and discuss the situation I would be glad to have you come in and talk it over.

Sincerely yours,
Harry S. Truman

CHAPTER FOUR

The Mass Media Presidency, 1953–1974

When Harry Truman was reelected in the surprise campaign of 1948, the news still reached most people by radio and newspaper. Truman himself had exhorted voters largely by a whistle-stop process using railroads and small-town stations, a practice that soon became defunct. The interstate highway system initiated during the Eisenhower administration, and commercial flights by jets, revolutionized travel, though not all for the better. Transmission technology made nationwide instant television viewing easy; soon satellite technology made the entire globe the White House's backyard. Every statement by a president became subject to instant coverage, and in time every president exploited that.

Seemingly avuncular letters from the White House to a child seldom again appeared in the news by accident—although some letters penned by Dwight Eisenhower, still naive about the reach of his mail, escaped staff scrutiny. In 1953, he had not been a civilian very long. (Harry Truman, too, had written some letters himself, stamped them at his personal expense, and posted them. In his early years as president he sometimes operated as a senator, working solo despite a staff.) While some presidential letters to young people remained personal in intent, others in increasingly communications-conscious administrations became cynically intended as public-relations releases. Such manipulation became especially blatant in the Johnson and Nixon years. Although an awareness of that potential had not escaped Kennedy aides, the brief "Camelot" presidency, in its surface ebullience, was especially reflected in JFK's instinctive feel for his youthful constituency.

DWIGHT D. EISENHOWER (1953–1961)
After 1953, policy goals and private presidential musings seldom ran on separate tracks in the Oval Office. Dwight Eisenhower had been so used to having

underlings handle his paperwork in the army, and employed the staff system so thoroughly while in the White House, that it is surprising to discover how frequently he wrote to children himself. Secretaries usually intervened at some level, yet the "Ike" flavor often emerges through the official prose. A grandfather figure to many children, Eisenhower was often treated as such in the letters he received from young people, one Texas boy even sending him a horned toad. In that case, the Secret Service involved itself, an official of its Protective Research Section writing the White House: "It looks like we'll have to set up a Wildlife Division if many youngsters hear of this. We don't mind bloodworms, goldfish, turtles, frogs or mice, but we have to draw the line somewhere between baby alligators and tarantulas." When a five-week-old donkey arrived at the White House, the gift of another boy, Eisenhower thanked the donor and had this symbol of the other political party presented to a camp for crippled children in Minnesota.

Confiding his personal political thoughts to a child in a way he seldom did to his peers, Ike wrote a long letter in response to a Massachusetts girl's request for his views for publication in her school newspaper. On second thought, perhaps, he decided it was not meant for print and had it stamped, "Confidential." The response must have daunted Ruth Ann Cuoto. When a boy in Indianapolis, addressing him as "Uncle Ike," asked the president what a sixth-grader should aspire toward, he responded seriously and signed his letter "Uncle Ike." When two sisters in Rhode Island wrote to him, "We think this is a free country, but is it really?" the president replied in a long, rambling letter combining memories of his boyhood in Kansas with his simplistic views on economics.

One youngster, a cerebral palsy victim, slept with a toy pistol by his pillow, defending Ike at night. When the president heard about it through a Red Cross worker, he was touched and wrote the boy a letter. Another boy wrote to the White House in advance of a presidential golfing weekend in Georgia to warn him of bad weather there. The weekend was past by the time the letter reached the White House, but Ike thanked him anyway. A girl in Richmond, Virginia, cut classes to attend a presidential appearance, and Ike penned an excuse note for her: "Could we not excuse the absence today of Isabel Ware? She was at a ceremony I attended." Another wrote sorrowfully from South Carolina that she had missed seeing the president when on a group tour of the White House, adding, "It's harder for me to write than it is for most 11-year-old girls. You see, I have cerebral palsy, and that makes me slow." Her letter went on for several laboriously handwritten pages, especially noting her appreciation for the kind White House guards who had carried her wheelchair around areas otherwise inaccessible to her. "Well," she concluded, it's taken me 'most all day to write this letter. I'm sorry 'cause it's so long. I do hope your secretary won't throw it away before you see it." Eisenhower saw it. Very little White House mail ends up in the wastebasket, whether or not the chief executive ever sees it. The president answered Harriet Lowe, "You are a nice little girl and I am sorry that my schedule was so full I could not see you that day." Very likely, too, Ike meant it.

Dwight D. Eisenhower to Master George Guanu

October 1, 1953

Dear George:

A friend of yours has just told Mrs. Eisenhower and me a wonderful story—that way up in Albany I have a small but courageous little bodyguard by day, and that my picture watches over you while you sleep. I am proud to have such a staunch defender, and I wanted you to know it.

Please tell your mother I hope very much the miracles of science will help you grow up to be strong and well—and as you grow a little older, know that my good wishes are always with you.

Sincerely,
Dwight D. Eisenhower

Dwight D. Eisenhower to John C. Nabors

May 2, 1955

Dear John:

Thank you for your nice letter—and for the horned toad that you sent me. Did you know that a long time ago I, too, lived in Texas? I agree with you that it is a wonderful state.

And I am glad you sent me your picture!

With best wishes to you, and to David, Billy and Jerry,

Sincerely,
Dwight D. Eisenhower

Dwight D. Eisenhower to John Bealieu

October 24, 1956

Dear John:

I can't tell you how pleased I was to receive the letter you wrote me recently in Braille. I certainly admire the skill that you must have had to master such a difficult art.

It was nice of you to send me a little speech to help win the election. Your good luck wishes for November mean a lot to me too, and I am very grateful to you for them. I wish I were able to write back to you in Braille also, but I am sure that one of your teachers will be happy to read this to you.

I hope you're enjoying your schoolwork and are taking advantage of the fine opportunity that you must have in Watertown. Many thanks again for being so thoughtful.

With best wishes,

Sincerely,
Dwight D. Eisenhower

Dwight D. Eisenhower to Robin and Terrill Scatena

Newport, Rhode Island
September 9, 1957

Dear Robin and Terrill:

I am complimented that you should write to me for an explanation of the things concerning our country and our government that are troubling your minds. None of the questions you ask can be answered in any single or simple statement. Each is so difficult and so many factors are involved that all citizens, including those that have been elected to governmental office, are sometimes puzzled in the attempt to find a solution that seems completely logical.

In spite of this, there are one or two facts that could well serve as a starting point for our thinking in these matters. Every single generation of Americans has had its own individual problems. Frequently the future has looked dark and discouraging—even to those young people who, normally, have far more courage and optimism than do their elders. A second fact is that America has not only successfully surmounted every crisis and period of discouragement, but her people have invariably gone forward to enjoy a fuller and better life spiritually, intellectually and materially.

The first thing that I would say, therefore, is that just as courage, fortitude and faith carried our forebears through their trials and difficulties, so will the same characteristics today and tomorrow bring to us solutions that are just and fair.

You are fearful about the depreciating value of the dollar; you correctly observe that unless we are successful in halting this trend, the insurance policies for which we pay today will not, some years later, buy the things and services and conveniences that they would today. The same applies to our pensions, to our savings accounts and to our savings bonds.

Many things combine to cause this cheapening of the dollar—or, to put it another way, this constant rise in the cost of things we need for daily living. In general the basic cause is that in recent years we have been trying to do too much too fast in terms of making and building things to sell. When too many Americans have too many plans in the economic field they want to carry out all at once, this creates pressure on resources—manpower, machines, materiel. In such a situation prices tend to rise.

The causes are of various kinds. One is the money spent by the government to provide all of the services that our population either needs or demands from the city, the state or the Federal government. Then, today, the Federal government has to spend an enormous amount—far more than half of all it collects—for the necessary defense of our country against the great Communist threat that faces all free countries today. Incidentally, it is part of this process of providing for the common security that occasions our expenditures that you hear called "foreign aid." We do not spend this money as charity for others. We spend in the sense of a premium on insurance policies against war, the most costly action in which any nation could indulge. War's cost, moreover, is paid in the lives of our young people, as well as in staggering amounts of money.

Another expenditure that cannot be escaped is the enormous interest we pay on our public debt. This interest must be paid fully and exactly on time, otherwise all of the war bonds in the hands of all of our people would collapse in value.

The rest of the money spent by the Federal government goes in general for the services that our people demand: aid to the states for helping take care of disabled and unemployed; aid to farmers in an effort to help them in the transition from an expanded wartime economy to a more stable peace time condition in which they can share more equitably in the national income; pensions and aid for veterans (in the amount of some billions of dollars); aid to all kinds of medical and health research, and many other things. Some of these things *could* be done by peoples and families for themselves. Or, if not by themselves, then by cities and states, rather than the Federal government. But by action of the Congress, some of these services are pressed upon the Federal government and as long as the people seem to think this is the best way to do it, then the price must be paid. I have been carrying on an effort to get more people to understand that more things can be done locally and with more efficiency by private citizens groups themselves. To that end I have set up a Federal-State Commission, to consider problems such as these.

Another cause of inflation is the rising cost of services. That is, if every workman gets higher wages for his services in excess of his increased efficiency, his employer is confronted with the need to raise the price of the things he sells. Consequently the dollar buys less and so we say it has been cheapened.

There are so many additional causes for rising prices or a cheapening dollar that eminent scholars and scientists have written whole books to describe them. More than this, some of these eminent scholars disagree with others, so that again we say that there just is no easy answer to the whole thing.

Nevertheless, there has been real progress made in recent years in slowing up this cheapening process. Usually the one or two decades immediately following the close of a great war have been an era . . . of rising prices and cheapening money. In any event, right after World War II we had a very marked period of this kind and for some years, with only one or two brief interruptions, the cost of living went up at the rate of over seven percent a year. Beginning in 1952, this process was slowed up sharply, and in the past five years, the total rise has been something between five and six percent *for the entire period*. In the past year and a half, we have seen most of this increase.

But your parents are correct in saying that we should strive—all of us—to keep a sound dollar. By this I mean to stop the inflation as rapidly as possible, without bringing upon us serious consequences in other directions, and thereafter to keep it under watchful control.

Every agency of the Federal government is striving to do this. But all history shows that it is not easy. We want our workmen to earn more. But whenever they obtain a pay raise that is in excess of the increased efficiency of the workmen then, as I pointed out before, we have another inflationary force.

And so it goes throughout our entire industry.

This letter is admittedly rather rambling, and you will realize that I have little opportunity either to reduce its length or make it more exact in its explanation. But I put these things down so that you will realize also that I do have some understanding of and do deplore the things that are bothering your minds today. And I repeat that all of us must do our best to stop the process.

Now—having said all this, I believe that America will remain free and that she will remain great; that you will have an opportunity to go to school, to fit yourselves for any careers of your own choosing; and that when you grow up you will be able to obtain and pay for a farm out of your earnings.

Again I would call attention to our history and the number of people of no great means who have gone to school and later achieved the top of their professions. In the section of Kansas from which I came, there were very few boys and girls who ever went to college who did not have to work outside of hours, while in school, in order to help defray their own expenses. Parents in that region, in those days, simply could not entirely pay their children's way through school. Three of my own brothers earned almost every cent of the money it cost them to obtain college degrees and all three graduated high in their classes.

So don't be discouraged about America. We do not have perfection, but the great opportunity that lies in front of each of us is to help bring this great and good country a little nearer to the perfection that all humans seek.

With best wishes to you both and to your parents.

Sincerely,
Dwight D. Eisenhower

Dwight D. Eisenhower to Billy Lee

The White House
March 24, 1960

Dear Billy:

Your letter poses a pretty big question, while at the same time I am pleased by the compliment implicit in your writing me.

But to try to answer you specifically: I would, if I were you, learn just as much about our country and the world as you possibly can; I would concentrate particularly on our history and what made America the great nation that it is. I would want to take all the science courses that are available in order more adequately to understand the developments that are certain to be made in the new era just opening up. And I would want to become proficient in one or more languages other than our own.

Perhaps you mean by asking what you should "aim toward," what profession I would advise. That I cannot begin to suggest, but if I were you I would simply try to be the best possible citizen of the United States. To this end you need to be informed on both domestic and international issues, and be aware of and understand the events that take place every day in the world around us. And as to what you should "do," I suspect you can do no better than live by the high precepts I know your parents have taught you.

If you do all of this, you will do more for me and for the rest of the people of our country than you possibly can now realize. I have no doubt that you will grow up to be a fine citizen in every respect.

With affectionate regard,

Sincerely,
Uncle Ike

Dwight D. Eisenhower to Ruth Ann Couto

April 13, 1960

PERSONAL AND CONFIDENTIAL

Dear Ruth Ann:

Thank you for your thoughtful letter. I am delighted to send you a personal reply, although I must request that you not publish it, as you suggest, in your school paper.

The question of whether we are "ahead" or "behind" the Russian government is one, of course, that engages the attention of a great number of people. It is a popular—and an easy—topic of conversation. Certainly it is evident that currently the Russians have greater power in their space engines, for instance, than have we; it is just as evident that in other areas we have demonstrated our own scientific superiority. But as to the basic question respecting our military strength, I assure you that it is not only adequate, but is deeply respected by the Soviets.

You ask whether there will be another World War. I can only repeat what I have said so many times; a war on a global basis, using the awesome weapons of which many countries are now capable, would, we all know, result in the annihilation of great portions of the earth. I am sure Mr. Khrushchev is as anxious as am I, and as are the leaders of other nations, to avoid such unthinkable catastrophe. My own unshakeable belief is that under these conditions our greatest danger is not military attack but exposure, throughout the free world, to Communist subversion and penetration.

I recognize the concern that you and your classmates have about these great issues; I hope you all appreciate the overwhelming advantage you have of living in freedom in a country where the individual's deeply held faith is paramount, as opposed to the atheistic doctrines of the Soviets. Moreover, I venture to suggest that your main job at the moment is to equip yourself, by education and all other possible means, to be an informed citizen of tomorrow; in so doing you and all the young people like you will be our country's greatest asset in making progress toward a durable peace in freedom.

With best wishes.

Sincerely,
Dwight D. Eisenhower

JOHN F. KENNEDY (1961–1963)

Eisenhower's rapport with young people was matched among presidents only by John Kennedy's. Whereas Eisenhower's approach, reflecting his years, was almost grandfatherly, in the tradition of a less-remembered former general in the White House, Benjamin Harrison, John Fitzgerald Kennedy, young in years and outlook, magnetized children. His wit and grace and charm, his two small children, his very closeness to their own generation captured the imagination of young people, who wrote to him in numbers that made personal responses impossible. At forty-two, he had already been a war hero, a congressman, and a senator. He had successfully campaigned against Eisenhower's heir apparent, Vice President Richard M. Nixon. From the very beginning of his abbreviated presidency in 1961, letters from children inundated the White House.

"Here is good news," a girl wrote to Kennedy. "I have decided to write you a different letter every day. This is letter number one." Another girl sent the first letter she typed on her new birthday-gift typewriter to the president. A boy suggested that Kennedy challenge Soviet premier Nikita Khrushchev to the Kennedy family favorite game of touch football, and another offered suggestions, to which JFK responded, on improving the Saturn rocket. Still another urged him to have a law passed—quickly—to lower the passing grade in arithmetic to 60. One boy thought that Kennedy was a terrific president except for his having publicly urged that everyone drink lots of milk. A Boy Scout wrote that he was keeping a scrapbook of everything that Kennedy had done every day since he became president. One day, however, was missing. "What exactly did you do on February 18, 1962? Please start with breakfast and go through supper."

A teenage girl wrote to the White House that it was "keen to have a President who isn't square" and labeled him with what history would now regard as an ironically candid understatement as "a real swinger." She had, of course, no idea how wrong she would be when she concluded, "Maybe they won't ever call you a swinger in the history books but to us you will always be the chief swinger of the USA." High school girls sent him their yearbooks to autograph, and at least one boy with a broken arm wrote (presumably with his other arm) to ask Kennedy to sign his cast. The logistics were left unclear.

Most children never received a JFK-signed reply. Kennedy's personally written letters usually went to children of politically connected parents, such as the sons of his friend and mentor John Kenneth Galbraith. Aide-concocted letters congratulated youngsters on a courageous act that had made the newspapers or on a confirmation, bar mitzvah, or other celebratory event. The president's time even for signing such letters was limited, and the mail continued to be enormous, with about five thousand letters received daily. To afford JFK a random sampling, every fiftieth letter was pulled from the pile and sent to the Oval Office. Sometimes Kennedy would go to the White House mailroom himself, extract a few supplementary letters from the sacks, and carry them to his desk. Letters that could be referred to governmental agencies or to a White House assistant for action were noted and forwarded by a clerk. Sometimes Kennedy, amused or intrigued by a letter, would have his personal secretary, Evelyn Lincoln, type a response, to which he often added a handwritten postscript, evidencing that the letter had not emerged from a signature machine.

After November 22, 1963, when Kennedy was assassinated while riding in an open car in a Dallas motorcade, the deluge of mail shifted tone, and Jacqueline Kennedy, who herself had been the recipient of hundreds of letters each day, began receiving sacks of condolence messages. Many were from children. One wrote for her class because she was the only student in it who owned a stamp. Another suggested that her late husband's profile be added to Mount Rushmore. Still another confided to Mrs. Kennedy that on November 22 her canary refused to sing.

Much of the Kennedy correspondence itself sings—with an enthusiasm felt on both sides. Despite the excessively self-conscious efforts of his successor to keep that mood alive, it would be buried with JFK.

John F. Kennedy to Master James Kenneth Galbraith

> Washington, D.C.
> January 26, 1961

Dear Jamie:

I understand that you were born in the last year of the last Democratic administration and are now celebrating your ninth birthday in these first two weeks of mine. I hope that the long Republican years have not hurt you too much, [and] that you will grow up to be at least as good a Democrat as your father but possibly of a more convenient size.

My best wishes for a happy birthday.

> Sincerely,
> John F. Kennedy

John F. Kennedy to Peter Woodard Galbraith

> Washington, D.C.
> March 28, 1961

Dear Peter:

I learn from your father that you are not very anxious to give up your school and friends for India. I think I know a little about how you feel. More than twenty years ago our family was similarly uprooted when we went to London where my father was ambassador. My younger brothers and sisters were about your age. They had, like you, to exchange old friends for new ones.

But I think you will like your new friends and your new school in India. For anyone interested, as your father says you are, in animals, India must have the most fascinating possibilities. The range is from elephants to cobras, although I gather the cobras have to be handled professionally. Indians ride and play polo so you will come back an experienced horseman.

But more important still, I think of the children of the people I am sending to other countries as my junior peace corps. You and your brothers will be helping your parents do a good job for our country and you will be helping out yourself by making many friends. I think perhaps this is what you will enjoy most of all.

My best wishes,

> Sincerely yours,
> John F. Kennedy

John F. Kennedy to John "Murphy" Chester

>Washington, D.C.
>August 30, 1961

Dear John:

To you, John, for campaigning so enthusiastically for me last Fall, I send my heartfelt thanks—a little late but nonetheless sincere.

I have heard that your tricycle covered a lot of ground in your neighborhood, and that you were a mighty convincing campaigner.

With my very best wishes,

>Sincerely,
>John F. Kennedy

John F. Kennedy to Remi Marcotte

>Washington, D.C.
>July 11, 1962

Dear Remi:

I have just learned about your heroic courage and coolheaded action in bringing your brothes and sisters—especially the baby—safely away from the flames which destroyed your home. Because I have great admiration for such a brave fellow as you, I want to add my word of commendation to those you have undoubtedly received from the Mayor of Corinth and thoughtful neighbors. Your parents can indeed be very proud of you.

With every good wish,

>Sincerely,
>John F. Kennedy

John F. Kennedy to John Carey, Jr.

>Washington, D.C.
>August 29, 1962

Dear Johnny:

Your friend Richard Gardner has passed on your letter with its interesting proposal about the Saturn rocket. He has also told me of the great interest you, Chipper and Douglas have in our outer space program and of your visit last spring to the United Nations Outer Space Committee.

I am very pleased that you and your brothers are following our space efforts so closely. The enthusiasm of young men like yourselves will assure the success of this program.

Sincerely,
John F. Kennedy

John F. Kennedy to Mark Aaron Perdue
Early in March 1963, the president received a letter from a boy in Fremont, California, who had been pondering St. Patrick's Day and apparently was aware of Kennedy's Irish ancestry.

Dear President Kennedy:
I like you very much. I am in special class in Fremont, California. I am 10 years old. Where do the little people live? Do they live under bushes? Do they have horses? Can only the Irish see them? Can you see them?
MARK AARON PERDUE

Washington, D.C.
March 14, 1963

Dear Mark:
I want to thank you for your nice letter. I enjoyed hearing from you and hearing about your school.

Your questions are quite pertinent, coming as they do just before St. Patrick's Day. There are many legends about the "little people," but what they all add up to is this: If you really believe, you will see them.

My "little people" are very small, wear tall black stovepipe hats, green coats and pants, and have long, white beards. They do not have horses. I have never been able to determine where they live. They are most friendly, and their message is that all the peoples of the world should live in peace and friendship.

Since you are interested in the Irish, I want to wish you a happy St. Patrick's Day.

Sincerely,
JOHN F. KENNEDY

LYNDON B. JOHNSON (1963–1969)

As an ambitious young congressman from Texas, Lyndon Baines Johnson used to choreograph elaborate replies from Franklin Roosevelt's White House by self-drafting them in advance to respond to his own letters and telegrams. With that slyness behind him, as president succeeding Kennedy, no one was more attuned than LBJ to the political usefulness of strategically released letters, even to (and from) children. From the first days of his presidency, he and his staff thought in terms of releasing advantageous correspondence to the press. Even when the White House itself did not make the correspondence available, the president's staff realized that many letters to young people would be offered by the proud parents to local media.

It became White House strategy to set aside for Johnson's signature those letters to which responses became indirect political gestures, or compliments to influential people, and those where LBJ's replies might enhance the presidential image in the press. Sometimes the mail from LBJ was an initiative rather than a response, for the White House was alerted only too often about the possibilities for a presidential letter from the politically faithful who had pipelines to the Executive Office staff. A boy in Congressman Pickle's district was in serious condition in a Texas hospital; the daughter of a member of a presidential board or commission was about to be married; or a White House assistant had plucked (or received) a clipping from a newspaper about a dying child who might be comforted by a letter from the president. Thus dozens of letters under the LBJ initials or signature went to pathetically ill children and to those on the verge of birthdays and other family events. The late President Kennedy's children received annual birthday messages, and Johnson took great pains to make them different.

Other LBJ letters to children established a presidential stance on a moral or social issue, doing missionary work for Johnson social programs. Some defended American involvement in Vietnam. Most were drafted by White House personnel, sometimes going through several texts by several staffers as versions traveled up the executive echelons to the Oval Office. The president would add his final touches, changing words or phrases where he wanted something more LBJ-like, and often adding a closing homily. In that fashion he made known, in a low-key but effective manner, his views on school prayer, the need for a strong defense posture, the importance of alleviating urban poverty, and other matters of concern to adults as well as children. Sometimes the letters had an immediate local impact—as when a girl in a Fort Worth slum wrote to the president about having nowhere to play but the front steps of her home, and asked for his support for her drive to create a girls' club. Not only did she receive a presidential letter, but the correspondence was forwarded to the appropriate Cabinet department for action, as well as to the Fort Worth *Star-Telegram*. Patty and her friends soon had a place to play.

Not every matter to which Johnson responded was of governmental concern. He thanked a North Carolina boy who sent him condolences on the death of the presidential beagle and offered a New Jersey boy a White House pup when the boy's own dog died. To a six-year-old girl in North Carolina who accidentally swallowed an "LBJ FOR THE USA" campaign button in 1964, he wrote, "I was certainly sorry to hear of your accident but pleased that it did not prove serious. The Democratic Party appreciates its enthusiastic supporters, but please, Vann, be more careful next time." The publicity was worth many paid political advertisements. To a Texas boy injured in a more serious accident, Johnson had his staff arrange for a note and a gift to be sent every other day until the boy was out of danger. The first was an autographed baseball.

Almost uniquely, no political implications were involved in the president's acknowledging a letter from fourteen-year-old Lyndon Johnson of Morwell, Australia, who achieved fame in the Melbourne area because of his name. His friends called him "Pres," the boy wrote, and enclosed a hometown newspaper clipping that noted that he was named for his mother (Lynette) and father (Don), rather than for a young senator from Texas whom few Australians had heard of in 1950. Still, LBJ warmed to the coincidence. "It is not often," he responded, "I get to put that name at both ends of a letter, and I find it quite an interesting experience."

Not every child's letter was answered with an LBJ signature. As in the case of John Kennedy's mail, the volume was enormous, and many were responded to by an assistant secretary with the chilly form text "In view of the overwhelming . . . demands upon his time . . ." Still, Johnson took his mail from young people very seriously, and his personnel probably spent more time on it than did the staff of any other president.

Lyndon B. Johnson to John F. Kennedy, Jr., and to Caroline Kennedy
On the evening of the day of President Kennedy's assassination in Dallas, his successor, having flown back to Washington from Texas with the presidential party that had been in the fatal motorcade, assembled the leadership of Congress to confer about the transition. Just before the meeting was to begin, the new president reached for two sheets of White House stationery and wrote out, in longhand, a brief message to each of the Kennedy children.

November 22, 1963
7:20 Friday Night

Dear John—

It will be many years before you understand fully what a great man your father was. His loss is a deep personal tragedy for all of us, but I wanted you particularly to know that I share your grief—

You can always be proud of him.

Affectionately,
Lyndon B. Johnson

Friday Night 7:30
November 22, 1963

Dearest Caroline—

Your father's death has been a great tragedy for the nation, as well as for you, and I wanted you to know how much my thoughts are with you at this time.

He was a wise and devoted man. You can always be proud of what he did for his country—

Affectionately
Lyndon B. Johnson

Lyndon B. Johnson to Miss Fern Butler

John F. Kennedy was assassinated in Dallas on November 23, 1963. Shortly afterward, the new president received a letter from an eleven-year-old Dallas girl, who assured him that she knew he would be a good president but worried that the city in which she lived—and Kennedy died—would have "a bad name" thereafter. Because of the delicacy of the question, and the opportunity the letter gave the new president to get on the record his feelings about any collective guilt Dallas citizens might be feeling—for the letter might be leaked to the press by the White House—Johnson's reply went through five complete drafts by his staff before he was satisfied with it.

The White House
Washington
December 5, 1963

My dear Fern:

Thank you for your very thoughtful and encouraging letter. President Kennedy's death has made all of us, young and old alike, sadder than anything we could have imagined.

What happens to the reputation of Dallas in the future depends on its citizens—particularly you and your cousin and all the children and young people of your city. If each and every one of you can learn the lesson of love which President Kennedy taught us—if we can all be a little more tolerant of each other and a little less ready to hate—if you can grow up learning to get along with and respect all kinds of people and to avoid saying mean things about them even where you do disagree—then your city and every city in this wonderful country of ours will be a better place in which to live.

Thank you again, Fern, for writing your President. I am so very grateful to you and I ask that you pray for me.

Sincerely,
Lyndon B. Johnson

Lyndon B. Johnson to Any Child
Early in his administration, Lyndon Johnson mandated to his staff that all presidential mail was "to be answered the day it is received," and although Lawrence O'Brien and others on his staff worked hard to respond quickly to correspondence from members of Congress and others with priority, there appeared no way to close the gap with letters of good will and congratulatory letters (especially during the 1964 campaign) and with letters to children. Horace Busby, anticipating the expected victory over Barry Goldwater, offered the president on November 1 two form-letter messages, one to adults (beginning "Your thoughtful personal message is deeply appreciated . . .") and one to children (beginning "I am very grateful to you for your message which Mrs. Johnson, Lynda and Luci have shared and enjoyed with me . . ."). But even before that, Chester V. Clifton of the White House staff had begun work on a different kind of response to children.

After consulting with Johnson on a method for managing most of the correspondence, Clifton came up with plans for a sixty-four-page all-purpose booklet with pictures and text, and opening with a letter from the president to children in general, complete to a facsimile autograph. The Curtis Publishing Company agreed to print 250,000 copies for the White House without cost, and the booklet, identified on the cover as "a Curtis publication" and titled ungrammatically *A Visit to the White House. The President Greets Young America—And Answers Their Questions,* featured a photo of Johnson reaching out to shake the outstretched hands of several dozen ethnically varied children. The letter from the president that greeted every child who opened the cover sounded less like LBJ than like his staff, and kept him remote from most of his young constituents, but at least each received a response that was a White House souvenir.

In one week in which statistics were kept shortly after the booklet became available, 4,449 letters and 4 postcards from children were received by the president (out of 61,211 total pieces of mail), requesting photos of Johnson or his dogs, his autograph, photos of his late predecessor, John Kennedy, or of the White House; asking for church contributions, funds for hardship cases, or White House tours; offering information of consequence only to the sender; or appealing for some particular presidential intercession. Of these, 2,262 were mailed copies of the booklet. The quarter of a million copies printed lasted longer than expected, as mail from children trickled off to a normal 2,000 units a week.

The White House
Washington

Dear friend,
Every month from every village, town and city thousands of letters come to me from boys and girls and young men and women, all over the country. These letters tell me a great deal about you, about your daily lives at home and in school, about your hopes and dreams and ambitions and your plans for the future. Many of you invite me to come to your cities and towns to visit your schools or to drop by your homes. These expressions of friendship are most heartwarming and I appreciate your thoughtfulness.

All of your letters are a source of pleasure and encouragement to me for they tell me what you are thinking. Many of you ask for information—you want to know more about our government and how it works, or about the White House, where I am now writing this letter, or about the Johnson family, the hobbies we have, the pets we enjoy. I know that you do not expect a direct answer, but when you ask for information the White House staff always tries to be as responsive and helpful as possible. That is why this little book has been published. I hope you will think of it as an answer to your questions, and that it will give you the sense of pride that comes from knowing that the White House is yours as well as mine.

Thank you for your letters. They make me proud of every boy and girl in the United States because they indicate your intense interest in this country we love so much. Your letters inspire me, and remind me that all of us working together will keep American strong and safe and free.

Cordially yours,
Lyndon B. Johnson.

Lyndon B. Johnson to Debbie L. Rae
Debbie Rae, twelve years old and blind, voiced her concern, in Braille, to the president that morning worship had been dropped by her school in Montclair, New Jersey, because of the Supreme Court's ruling in the matter. She wanted to be sure, she wrote, that God would watch over her in school, in particular when she was doing arithmetic, and wanted his help in restoring prayer to the public schools. Johnson's letter was put into Braille to be forwarded to her.

The White House
April 17, 1964

My dear Debbie:
I want you to know how grateful I am for your nice letter.

I have the feeling that God is looking after you. Even though you do not have morning worship at your school, God, who marks the fall of every sparrow, will hear the prayers in your heart.

Very frequently, Debbie, your own heart is the biggest church in the world. As long as you keep the faith, you need not worry.

My warmest best wishes to you,

Sincerely,
Lyndon B. Johnson

Lyndon B. Johnson to Miss Leota Teale
Twelve-year-old Leota Teale of Des Moines, Iowa, wrote the president that when he went on television to announce his escalation of American involvement in Vietnam, she was less scared about her father, who was in the

National Guard and might be called to wartime duty, than that she herself would die in a new war. Now, she confided, she was ashamed of her fears and understood that the United States wanted peace but could not tolerate aggression. It was exactly Johnson's own preachment, and he warmed to a reply, changing "reasonable men" in his staff draft to "reasonable people," since he was writing to a girl, but making another change that demonstrated that, like many students of Leota's age and older, he was not sure that *its* could ever be written without an apostrophe. His secretary typed it as incorrectly as LBJ penned it.

Washington, D.C.
August 13, 1964

Dear Leota:

I wanted to thank you with a personal note for the very warm letter you sent me.

Let me say first that there is no reason for you to feel ashamed. All reasonable people fear war—especially in this nuclear age. The ability to calmly and realistically face this danger is the mark of true courage. The most important challenge of these times is for our nation to resolutely use this courage to deter or punish aggression. Peace can be maintained only if our adversaries fully understand our will and our determination to champion freedom for all men. This is why we maintain the most powerful military forces in mankind's history. If we are to succeed in keeping the peace, this great power must be used in the most careful, precise and responsible manner.

The quest for peace is our most important goal. It's achievement is essential, so that fine young people like yourself can grow up with the liberty and dignity which is the birthright of every American.

Sincerely,
Lyndon B. Johnson

Lyndon B. Johnson to Nicholas Osborne

The White House
May 30, 1966

Dear Nicholas:

I learned today about the saddest tragedy that could happen to a little boy. I love dogs, so I can understand the grief you felt because your best friend passed from you.

Please let your President try, in a small way, to help you blot out your unhappiness. If you like, I will send you another friend who, I think, will find in you the love that you gave to Snoopy, who has now gone away. I believe he will love you and be loyal to you because I have a feeling this little beagle is especially partial to a four year old boy. Please let me know if you would like to have this new friend.

May God bless you, Nicholas. I will wait to hear from you.

Sincerely,
Lyndon B. Johnson

Lyndon B. Johnson to Miss Dorothy Emma Brown
Dottie Brown, a poor, uneducated sixteen-year-old girl who apparently lived alone on her earnings, worked for the Neighborhood Youth Corps in Portland, Maine. Her sensitive yet semiliterate letter to President Johnson about her experiences led the White House staff to explore the idea of publicizing a presidential reply, for, as a Youth Corps official put it to an assistant presidential press secretary, "lack of any real communication between the affluent and the poor is, essentially, the biggest obstacle in overcoming poverty." But before a letter was drafted and released, Johnson asked the FBI to run a check on Dottie Brown to make sure this was not a hoax. Then the Portland *Press Herald*—the largest newspaper in Maine—was sent copies of both sides of the correspondence, and a front-page story, with photo of Dorothy Emma Brown, appeared on Sunday, July 17, 1966, in the *Sunday Telegram and Press Herald*. It had taken two and a half months from Dottie's letter to that point, but the story was not over, for Dottie had never received the original letter (she had moved from rooming house to rooming house), and after postal inspections failed to find it, and even Sen. Edmund Muskie had intervened on her behalf, she was sent a White House copy.

5/2/66

Dear President Johnson,

My name is Dorothy Emma Brown. I live at 12 Wescott St. Portland Maine. Im 16. I live alone. I have been living alone for at least a year now. I had a hard life when I was young.

Im in the NYC. I work at the Y.W.C.A. I like my work very much. I do work with children. that's the most important part in my job.

Yesterday, my councilor Mr. Franciose and Mrs. Kimball put me on a spical mission. The mission was going around to different houses and trying to get the parent's to sign the form for their children ages 5 for the head start program.

I have to amit it wasn't easy. I just couldn't believe the thing's I saw.

I went to one house on salem st. The woman had 5 children, all little one's. their were feather's all over the place and it looked like they got the furniture out of the dump, the kid's were running and crying, and the mother looked like she had a six pack, what I mean is she looked like she been drinking.

One of the kid's was sitting on the floor trying to get in a bottle of pill's. their was two of the kid's out sid fighting. I was trying to make the baby laugh, but she just look at me and then turn over in the crib and went to sleep.

I couldn't stand it and so I went out side while she (the mother) was signing the paper. I told the kid's to stop fighting and then I went in side the house, took the bottle of pills away from the little girl, check her mouth and went out.

Boy! was that place cold. I felt like taking the kid's and run.

There was another place on pine street. I felt sorry for those kid's too. their must have been eight, know father, all little one's, rate up to eight year's old.

They were the cutest kid's I have ever seen. I talk to them and you can tell their hurt. their mother was very mean to them.

One of the boy's was sick of should I say retarded. He started coming over to me and his mother belted him. I told his mother their wasn't know [reason] for that, and she said he was alway's in her way. I told her if she didn't want them why that she have them.

I know that wasn't right for me to say that. I know it was none of my business, but Im interested in kid's so I think it is my business.

There was another Place on congress street by munjoy hill. She had about 9 kid's, for what Ive sen she looked like she was about 60. She had the shakes for maybe it's because of drinking. I wouldn't be surpise at all.

The funerture look's like it came from the grand central dump. Im not joking either it was torn and had hole's all through it.

the kid's looked like they came from overseas somewhere. A little girl of about two climb on top of a table or what was left of it, and going to jump. I caught her just in time.

I could go on and on but I think I gave an idea how a lot of people live, in Portland.

If there is anyway I could help these children I would, and I think the N.Y.C. kid's would to.

I don't understand why the President of the united States help these other countrie's when he can't even help his own.

Well, I think I made my self clear in a lot of thing's I wanted to say.

I sure can see that I had a hard life, but their's people that is worse off than I am.

Sincerely your's
Dottie Brown

The White House
Washington
June 29, 1966

Dear Dottie,

I was deeply impressed by your letter about your work with the Neighborhood Youth Corps and your experience in signing up children for the Head Start program in Portland.

It is obvious that you have acquired an important lesson that some people never learn.

The lesson is that regardless of how hard life seems at times—and you have known how hard it can be—conditions can be even worse for others.

I think you would agree with me that our country is the greatest on earth—and that never before have Americans enjoyed such prosperity. That is why I am so grateful to young people like you for giving of your time to help make life a little bit better for your neighbors.

I am glad to hear that you have been going to night school. Keep it up, Dottie, because nothing is more important than adequate education in preparing for the years ahead.

We are depending on citizens of your determination to make this a nation in which some day there will be no such thing as the poverty which caused you to write to me.

Sincerely
LBJ

Lyndon B. Johnson to Stephen James Cook
Stephen's big brother, William, was killed by small-arms fire in Vietnam on December 17, 1966. If the president had not escalated the war and put Americans in the front lines instead of South Vietnamese, Stephen suggested in his childish scrawl, his brother would still have been alive to celebrate his next birthday in January.

The White House
December 30, 1966

Dear Stephen:

I was touched by your letter and wanted to send you a personal acknowledgment in the hope that it might bring you some small comfort.

You must have loved your brother very much. I can only say that grief is something your President understands and shares with you.

I did not know William, but from what I know of brave men like him I expect he returned your love and in large measure gave his life for it.

He fought for you and every young person whose future is to grow in peace and freedom. He fought to keep his other brothers and sisters safe—the boys, girls and families of South Vietnam, Asia and the world.

I hope you do think of these people as part of your family. I feel William would have wanted you to share your love for him with every member of the human family. That is the way to end war—with love and understanding among men.

I am proud of your brother. I hope you will be proud of his cause and take it up. So many men have died, all through history, to give you that chance. You can make their sacrifices meaningful by making your life an example for the men of your generation, and all men to come.

God keep you in that good purpose.

Sincerely,
LBJ

Lyndon B. Johnson to Patrick Lyndon Nugent

June 22, 1968

Dear Lyn,

Today is a very special day for both of us. It marks your first year of life and my first year as a grandfather. It is a role which has given me more joy than any other and it would not have been possible without you.

There is a great deal of talk about the generation gap these days. Perhaps when you are old enough to read this letter, it will have all disappeared. Right now, I do not fear it. I salute it. For the generation gap between us creates those very special feelings that come when I hold your hand in mine, or jiggle you on my knee.

That sort of behavior won't last too long, I'm afraid. It will be replaced too soon by demeanor more fitting to a senior citizen and his grandson. As the gap in years diminishes between us, we will shake each other by the hand; I will still call you Lyn but in a different voice; and you will sprinkle your conversations with me liberally with 'Sirs.'

But let us make a pact, here and now, never to forget inwardly these days, these emotions, this warmth and trust we share, no matter how custom in years to come may restrict our outward behavior and expression.

You are my link to the future; you are also my link to the present. In you and through you I have an even deeper sense of responsibility to all the other children, their mothers and fathers and their grandparents, not just in America but throughout the world.

And I devoutly wish for them the happy, fruitful, and ennobling life I wish for you—a life free of war, poverty, disease, and inner darkness; an end to the conditions that separate fathers from their families on happy occasions like this.

This I wish, and with God's help, to this I declare myself. In the time left to me, I will do everything in my power to make it so. Not just for us in our times—but for all time.

God bless you, grandson.

With love,
Lyndon B. Johnson

RICHARD M. NIXON (1969–1974)

Of the Richard Nixon letters that have become accessible, few are to children. According to his aides, he was an unusually effective writer to young people and wrote many letters to them on his own, after hours and without staff intervention. His letter of consolation to young Terry Eagleton bolsters that contention, as does his response to Jonathan Schorr. Nixon was also attuned to the political implications of a letter he could release to the press, and some of his carefully phrased letters to children about the Vietnam dilemma demonstrate that side of his personality. Some of his opportunities to make political points with a letter were deliberately unused when he employed the telephone frequently to do what a personal letter might have done concretely but less warmly. To his credit, for example, he telephoned young Teddy Kennedy, Jr., at the hospital when the son of one of Nixon's chief adversaries was recovering from surgery on a cancerous leg. His letters to John Kennedy's children on their visiting the White House for the first time since their father's death are marvels of sensitivity and accordingly close this collection. Whether ogre or victim as president, Richard Nixon remained an extraordinarily complex man.

Richard M. Nixon to Caroline and John Kennedy

With the official portraits of the late president and of Mrs. Kennedy about to be hung in the White House, Nixon had the former first lady and her children, Caroline (thirteen) and John, Jr. (ten), flown from New York for a secret dinner. The date was February 3, 1971. Jackie Kennedy had asked for the private visit rather than have to go through a public ceremony. Afterward, the children wrote thank-you notes to the Nixons, and the president responded separately to each.

> *Dear Mr. President*
> *Dear Mrs. Nixon*
> I can never thank you more for showing us the White House.
> I really liked everything about it. You were so nice to show us everything.
> I don't think I could remember much about the White House but it was really nice seeing it all again.
> When I sat on Lincoln's bed and wished for something, my wish really came true. I wished that I would have good luck at school. I loved all the pictures of the Indians and the ones of all the Presidents.
> I also really liked the old pistols.
> I really really loved the dogs. They were so funny. As soon as I came home my dogs kept on sniffing me. Maybe they remember the White House.
> The food was the best I have ever had. The shrimp was by far the best I have ever tasted.
> And the steak with the sauce was really good.
> And I have never tasted anything as good as the souffle . . . was the best I ever tasted.
> I really liked seeing the President's office and the cabinet room a lot. Thank you so much again.
> *Sincerely,*
> *John Kennedy*

Dear Mrs. Nixon,

Thank you so much for the incredible tour. You were so nice to do it and I just love everything about the house. All the rooms are so lovely and it was so sweet of you to take us around so specially. I just love your dogs. King Timaho is beautiful and the others are so cute. The dinner was delicious. Your Swiss chef is the best thing that ever came out of Switzerland except maybe the chocolate. Your daughters were so nice to me, I had such a good time and it was so nice to see it all again. The President was so nice (repeat—repeat) to take so much time out of his schedule. Please thank him.

The portraits were hung so nicely. You made them look so good. Everything was just perfect and everyone was so nice. Please thank them all for me, Allen, John, the one who met us at the door, and everyone else. But thank you and your family most of all. I will really never forget it.

Love
Caroline

P.S. The plane is fantastic and the candy is wonderful. Sgt. Simmons is great and so is the pilot. All I seem to be saying is so nice, fantastic, thank you, but it is all I can say.

Several weeks later, Nixon wrote warm letters back:

Dear Caroline—

I want you to know how much we appreciated your letter after our visit at The White House—We did not share the contents with anyone but our Swiss Chef was deeply touched when I told him that you had written so generously about his culinary creations.

I recall that you told us your favorite subject was history but that a poor teacher this year had somewhat dampened your interest. I know a teacher can make a great difference but I hope your enthusiasm for history continues.

History is the best foundation for almost any profession—but even more important you will find the really most fascinating reading as you grow older is in history and biography.

As far as the teacher is concerned I recall that some of the teachers I thought at the time were the worst (because they graded so hard) were actually the best in retrospect. I would guess you are an exceptionally good student and I hope the teacher doesn't discourage you!

Mrs. Nixon, Tricia and Julie join me in sending our best. You will always be welcome in this House.

Richard Nixon

Dear John—

We all greatly enjoyed your letter and we were particularly happy that your visit to the White House where you lived as a very young boy left pleasant memories.

I will let you in on a little secret with regard to our dogs. *Usually* Mrs. Nixon—for obvious reasons—will not allow them to come to the second floor. So you can see that your visit was a special treat for them (and for me!—I don't worry so much about what happens to the furniture).

I was glad your wish which you made on the Lincoln bed came true—when you need another one like that—come back to see us. You will always be welcome in This House.

Sincerely
Richard Nixon

Richard M. Nixon to Terry Eagleton

Just after Democratic presidential nominee George McGovern had dropped Sen. Thomas Eagleton from the vice presidential slot on his ticket, worried about public reaction to revelations of Eagleton's having had recovered from a bout of depression that had required shock therapy, a photograph of Eagleton and his son, taken on a visit to the White House a year earlier, was published in *Life* magazine.

Remembering that he had been pressured to "get off the ticket" in 1952 but had survived the episode with his "Checkers speech" on television, while presidential candidate Eisenhower had stood by noncommittally, Nixon reacted with a handwritten letter to young Terry Eagleton. As William Safire wrote: "It was not done for the publicity—there was none." In his reply to the President, Terry Eagleton wrote, "Do you know what my Dad said when he read your letter? He said, 'It's going to make it all the tougher to talk against Nixon.'" "That thought might have occurred to the President," Safire added, "but . . . the gesture was Nixon doing a natural, thoughtful thing."

Personal
THE WHITE HOUSE
WASHINGTON

August 2, 1972

Dear Terry—

When I saw the picture in *Life* a week ago I was reminded of our meeting at the White House when your father introduced you to me after I signed the Construction Safety Bill. I thought you might like to have a copy of the White House Photographer's picture of that meeting.

I realize these past few days have been very difficult ones for you and the members of your family. Speaking as one who understands and respects your father's decision to continue to fight for his party's nominees and against my administrative policies, I would like to pass on to you some strictly personal thoughts with regard to the ordeal your father has undergone.

Politics is a very hard game. Winston Churchill once pointed out that "politics is even more difficult than war, because in politics you die many times; in war you die only once."

But in those words of Churchill we can all take some comfort. The political man can always come back to fight again.

What matters is not that your father fought a terribly difficult battle and lost. What matters is that in fighting the battle he won the admiration of foes and friends alike because of the courage, poise and just plain guts he showed against overwhelming odds.

Few men in public life in our whole history have been through what he has been through. I hope you do not allow this incident to discourage or depress you.

Years later you will look back and say "I am proud of the way my dad handled himself in the greatest trial of his life."

Sincerely

Richard Nixon

P.S. I hope your arms are completely healed.

RN

Richard M. Nixon to Jonathan Schorr

Jonathan Schorr, then nearly seven, prepared and illustrated his own "get well soon" card when the former president's hospitalization was in the news. It was forwarded to Nixon by the boy's father, Daniel Schorr, who was at the time a CBS television newscaster not known for friendly feelings toward San Clemente's best-known resident.

La Casa Pacifica
San Clemente, California
May 28, 1975

PERSONAL

Dear Jonathan,

Your illustrated get-well message, which came to me through the courtesy of your father when I was in the hospital last Fall, brought me much pleasure, and all the more so because you had taken the time to fashion it yourself. Even at this late date, I wanted you to know of my appreciation for your thoughtfulness and concern at that time.

If only you and the other young people of your generation can grow up and mature without experiencing the horrors of war, my greatest goal during my years in the White House will have been achieved. Perhaps you will choose to follow in your father's footsteps, and, if you do, I trust I will live long enough to observe you on television.

With every good wish for the years ahead,

Sincerely,
Richard Nixon

AFTERWORD:
POST-NIXON, 1974–

The letter as a medium of communication no longer has the urgency in private life that it once had. Even less has it survived in public life, especially in the busiest and most public office in the land. Telephone and electronic mail have replaced hard copy, although the option exists to turn almost anything electronic into printed copy. Richard Nixon telephoned young Ted Kennedy when he was hospitalized, and Nixon's successor, Gerald Ford, telephoned, rather than wrote to, the unhappy Connecticut teenager whose car struck the presidential limousine during a motorcade. His form letters responding to children, which often had nothing to do with the subject about which they had written, began "Dear Young Friend." When it came to letters from the Ford White House, bland and mechanical responses were the rule.

Jimmy Carter, who followed, began idealistically by responding personally to a carefully selected twenty of the weekly seventy thousand letters then being received, a number and a system that almost eliminated the possibility of any direct communication with the children who were beginning to write to 1600 Pennsylvania Avenue by the classroom-load. Instead, he offered young writers, whatever the inquiry, a LBJ-like form letter that included illustrations and began "The White House is my family's home while I'm President, but it belongs to all the American people. To tell you more about it, I've asked my family and friends to put together this booklet, 'The White House—it's your house, too.'" His staff assistants sometimes sent such boilerplate as "President Carter has asked me to reply to your recent message and express his appreciation for your kind words and good wishes"—this even to unread critical letters.

In Ronald Reagan's and George Bush's administrations, similar form letters made it unnecessary to reply with any specificity, and newspapers sometimes made fun of the disjunction when reported to them. Reagan even read to Congress a letter from an eight-year-old wishing him well after an attempt on his life: "I hope you get well quick or you might have to make a speech in your pajamas." The letter had been picked for the purpose by Reagan's chief speechwriter from a mountain of solicitous mail. Reagan's response was in his speech, which may have been all for the best, as swollen White House staffs might have bungled the answer. In part, the presidential shyness about responding to children has been a defense mechanism, as more and more teachers have been using a letter to the president as a writing assignment, assuming that employing the White House as an address will motivate students. (The letter to Reagan came from a class project at a school in Rockville Center, New York.)

Administration after administration, such classroom products are sent on to Washington, creating logistics problems in the White House mailroom. If teachers don't think of doing it, someone else will do so for them. Since 1981 (the year, coincidentally, of the Reagan shooting), the scholastic publication *Weekly Reader* has asked schoolchildren from kindergarten to middle school to tell the president what they most want him to do, and in 1997 the children responded with ninety-three thousand letters, poems, drawings, quilts, photographs, audiotapes, and videotapes, which were presented to Bill Clinton. One child told him, "Guns scare kids. We are scared of coming to school." Another wrote, "I want to take gangs off the streets so there are less robberies." A third-grader drew a tearful girl clutching a doll, and captioned it, "Hear the crys of the children. Please stop the abuse." Another third-grader wrote, "This is the only planet we can live in, and other things won't matter if we don't have our environment." A fourth-grader urged, "Please help protect the animals of our world. Don't let them become history." Many classes collaborated on a letter, one fourth grade drawing a football field and listing its suggestions between the yard markers. One proposed, "When a tree is cut down, replace it with a new tree." "Our class voted," another fourth-grade class wrote to Clinton, "that the President's goal should be to create a world where there are no homeless people and no starving children."

Although the ideas of young people, so voiced, are a useful sounding board, the mass efforts, now unstoppable, also suggest an unrealistic understanding of presidential powers. The bully pulpit has to promote the possible, and the president, while a global leader, is not the president of the world. Such assignments awaken children to the outside world but evoke unrealistic expectations and flood the White House with unanswerable mail.

If there is anything left of the father figure in future occupants of the White House—and technology does not distance writer and addressee even further—we may expect many more illuminating letters in response to the young friends of future presidents. The problem will be to extract the letters that should be answered from the burgeoning mass of mail and, now, e-mail, that arrives at 1600 Pennsylvania Avenue daily. The letters from any American president's least-known constituency will keep emerging, and how to renew contact with that generation will remain each new president's challenge.

SOURCES

GEORGE WASHINGTON

Anastasia de Lafayette to George Washington, June 12, 1784, reproduced with permission from the manuscript in the Cornell University Library

Other letters from the *Centennial Edition* of Washington's writings, ed. John C. Fitzpatrick, as reproduced in *Affectionately Yours, George Washington. A Self-Portrait in Letters of Friendship*. Edited by Thomas J. Fleming. New York: W. W. Norton, 1967

JOHN ADAMS

Early letters from *Adams Family Correspondence,* IV. Edited by L. M. Butterfield and Marc Friedlander. Cambridge: Harvard University Press, 1973

Post-presidential letters from the microfilm of the letterpress copies produced by the Massachusetts Historical Society, and quoted by permission of the Massachusetts Historical Society

THOMAS JEFFERSON

The Papers of Thomas Jefferson. Edited by Julian P. Boyd and others. Princeton: Princeton University Press, 1950

The Writings of Thomas Jefferson. Edited by Paul Leicester Ford. New York: G. P. Putnam's Sons, 1892–1899

The Family Letters of Thomas Jefferson. Edited by Edwin M. Betts and James Beer, Jr. Columbia, Missouri: University of Missouri Press, 1966

JOHN QUINCY ADAMS

From the microfilm of the letterpress copies produced by the Massachusetts Historical Society, quoted by permission of the Massachusetts Historical Society

ANDREW JACKSON
Correspondence of Andrew Jackson. Edited by John Spencer Bassett. Washington, D.C.: Carnegie Institution, 1929. Corrected and supplemented from the original manuscripts in the Library of Congress

Letter to Alice Egerton, October 25, 1842, from the manuscript in the collection of Ronald von Klaussen and reproduced with his permission

MARTIN VAN BUREN
Photocopies of letters in the Papers of Martin Van Buren, furnished by George W. Franz when curator of the collection, from the Pennsylvania State University (PSU) Libraries*

JOHN TYLER
Letters and Times of the Tylers. Edited by Lyon Gardiner Tyler, Richmond, Virginia: Whittet & Shepperson, 1884, 1894

JAMES POLK
Photocopies and typescripts of letters in the Tennessee State Library and Archive, and in the Library of Congress, furnished by Wayne Cutler, editor of *The Correspondence of James K. Polk*

MILLARD FILLMORE
From photocopies of letters in the Penfield Library, State University of New York at Oswego, furnished by Donald W. Barden, archivist

FRANKLIN PIERCE
From photocopies of letters in the collections of the New Hampshire Historical Society, Concord, New Hampshire, furnished by Jean G. Johnson, assistant archivist

JAMES BUCHANAN
Letters to James Buchanan Henry from copies in the Historical Society of Pennsylvania, furnished by John Guertler, Manuscripts Department

Letter to Maria Weaver from the original manuscript in the PSU Libraries, furnished by Charles W. Mann, director of special collections

Letters to Harriet Lane from George Ticknor Curtis, *The Life of James Buchanan*, New York: Harper and Brothers, 1883

---

*All references to archivists are to the suppliers of documents at the time of receipt.

ABRAHAM LINCOLN
From *The Collected Works* of Abraham Lincoln, IV–VII. Edited by Roy P. Basler for the Abraham Lincoln Historical Association. New Brunswick, New Jersey: Rutgers University Press, 1953

ANDREW JOHNSON
From the Johnson-Bartlett Collection, Greeneville, Tennessee, manuscript copies furnished by LeRoy P. Graf, coeditor, *The Papers of Andrew Johnson*

ULYSSES S. GRANT
Letter to Nell Grant from *An Address Delivered by Frank H. Jones before the Chicago Historical Society at the 100th Celebration of the Birth of General Ulysses S. Grant, Thursday, April Twenty-Seventh, Nineteen Twenty-Two*. Chicago: The Chicago Historical Society, 1922. Furnished by John Y. Simon, The Ulysses S. Grant Association

Mock commission to Willie Hillyer, and letter to Ulysses S. Grant, Jr., from *The Papers of Ulysses S. Grant, III* and *XX*. Edited by John Y. Simon. Carbondale, Illinois: Southern Illinois University Press, 1972, 1995

RUTHERFORD B. HAYES
Letters to "Ruddy" (Rutherford Platt Hayes) from photocopies in the Rutherford B. Hayes Library, Fremont, Ohio, furnished by Watt P. Marchmain, director

Additional letters from the *Diary and Letters of Rutherford Birchard Hayes, IV.* Edited by Charles R. Williams. Columbus, Ohio: Ohio State University Press, 1925

JAMES A. GARFIELD
From the Library of Congress microfilms of the Garfield Papers

CHESTER ALAN ARTHUR
From the Library of Congress microfilms of the Arthur Papers

GROVER CLEVELAND
From the Library of Congress microfilms of the Cleveland Papers

BENJAMIN HARRISON
Letter to his grandson Ben from the Indiana Historical Society, Indianapolis, Indiana, photocopy furnished by Leona T. Altig, manuscripts librarian

Letter to Elizabeth Llida Jones, from the manuscript at the President Benjamin Harrison Memorial Home, Indianapolis, Indiana, photocopy furnished by Katherine Svarzkopf, archivist

WILLIAM McKINLEY
From the Library of Congress microfilms of the McKinley Papers

THEODORE ROOSEVELT
Letters to his children and to Sarah Butler and Jimmy Garfield from *Theodore Roosevelt's Letters to His Children*. Edited by Joseph Bucklin Bishop. New York: Scribner, 1919
Letter to Marjorie Sterrett from *The Letters of Theodore Roosevelt, VIII*. Edited by Elting E. Morison and others. Cambridge, Massachusetts: 1954. This edition, although ostensibly complete, does not contain some of the non-family letters to children, yet some of the family letters are more complete than in the Bishop edition.

WILLIAM H. TAFT
From the Library of Congress microfilms of the Taft Papers

WOODROW WILSON
From the Library of Congress microfilms of the Wilson Papers

WARREN G. HARDING
From microfilm copies furnished by the Ohio Historical Society, Ohio Historical Center, Columbus, Ohio, Charles A. Isetts, librarian

CALVIN COOLIDGE
Letters to his son John Coolidge furnished in photocopy by the late John Coolidge, Plymouth, Vermont

HERBERT HOOVER
Letters from the presidential years furnished in photocopy by the Herbert Hoover Presidential Library, West Branch, Iowa, by Robert Wood, assistant director
Letters from the post-presidential years from Herbert Hoover, *On Growing Up: letters to American boys & girls*. Edited by William Nichols. New York: Morrow, 1949, which omits childrens' surnames to protect their privacy

FRANKLIN DELANO ROOSEVELT

Letters to and from Roosevelt from the originals and from carbon copies in the Franklin D. Roosevelt Presidential Library, Hyde Park, New York, furnished by Joseph Marshall, acting director. Staff memoranda regarding FDR's letter to young King Peter of Yugoslavia is also from Hyde Park.

HARRY S. TRUMAN

Letters to and from Truman from the originals and carbon copies in the Harry S. Truman Presidential Library, Independence, Missouri

Letter to Margaret Truman is published in Margaret Truman, *Harry S. Truman.* New York: Morrow, 1973

DWIGHT D. EISENHOWER

Letters to and from Eisenhower from photocopies of manuscripts and carbon copies in the Dwight D. Eisenhower Presidential Library, Abilene, Kansas, furnished by Don W. Wilson, acting director

JOHN F. KENNEDY

Letters to and from JFK are from photocopies in the John F. Kennedy Presidential Library, Boston, Massachusetts, furnished by Joan Hoopes, archivist

LYNDON B. JOHNSON

Letters to and from LBJ are from originals and copies in the Lyndon B. Johnson Presidential Library, Austin, Texas

RICHARD M. NIXON

Letter to Terry Eagleton from William Safire, *Before the Fall: an inside view of the pre-Watergate White House.* Garden City, New York: Doubleday, 1975

Letter to Jonathan Schorr furnished in photocopy by his father, Daniel Schorr

Letters to and from the Kennedy children are from copies in the Richard M. Nixon Library & Birthplace, Yorba Linda, California

POST-NIXON

Data and documents are from the collection of the editors

G. Washington

Th. Jefferson

Andrew Jackson

A. Lincoln

Franklin D. Roosevelt